The Blessing
of a Ginkgo Tree

A Collection of Devotions
by the Clergy
of Christ Episcopal Church

authorHOUSE®

AuthorHouse™
1663 Liberty Drive
Bloomington, IN 47403
www.authorhouse.com
Phone: 1-800-839-8640

First published by AuthorHouse 11/18/2010

ISBN: 978-1-4567-0080-5 (e)
ISBN: 978-1-4567-0079-9 (sc)

Library of Congress Control Number: 2010916869

Printed in the United States of America

Certain stock imagery © Thinkstock.

This book is printed on acid-free paper.

Introduction

The first e-devotions were intended to be only a four-week Advent series, but by the time Christmas came, it was clear that the e-devotion was a wonderful way for the scattered people of Christ Church midweek to share a moment of spiritual reflection together.

E-devotions soon became a way to stay connected, to tell stories of ministry and grace, to encourage hope in Christ's power to heal and renew, to respond to current events from the context of faith, and to reflect on the seasons of the church year and the seasons of life.

One doctor in our parish told me that when he sees the e-devotion appear on his Blackberry on busy Wednesdays, he takes a moment apart from the queue of patients to read it and be refreshed. Other parishioners say the e-devotion heightens their awareness of God's presence and work around them. Some like how it makes them think more deeply about what they believe and what it means to be Jesus' disciple in everyday life. Many say they appreciate the unique voice of each member of the clergy writing the e-devotions.

Standing beside the front door of Christ Church is a stately ginkgo tree that is transformed each autumn into a visible symbol of the glory of God. Each fall the tree blesses all who pass by it as surely as a prayer or benediction could. It is our hope that this collection of e-devotions offers a blessing to readers and provides time for sitting under the shade of God's love and care.

The Rev. Lisa Saunders
September 2010

Editors' Note

When Lisa Saunders asked our committee to pursue the idea of publishing a collection of the Christ Church e-devotions, we began with enthusiasm. Soon, though, we realized what a difficult task we had on our hands. As we passed around copies of several years' worth of e-devotions, we remembered our favorites and discovered others that we had somehow missed or forgotten. It was tough to select some and set others aside. This book is the product of our collective sense of which of them would inspire, challenge, and comfort readers within our parish as well as our neighbors near and far, both now and in the years to come.

We are grateful to the Christ Church clergy for the blessing of these e-devotions: our Rector, the Rev. Henry H. "Chip" Edens, III; our Interim Rector in 2005-06, the Rev. Nicholson B. White; our Associate Rectors, the Rev. Martha H. Hedgpeth, the Rev. W. Verdery Kerr, the Rev. John M. Porter-Acee , III, and the Rev. Lisa G. Saunders; and our former Associate Rector the Rev. Julia W. Boyd (now Mitchener).

Some e-devotions were edited slightly for space or context.
You will note that our clergy signed their e-devotions in different ways at different times. Rather than enforce conformity in the editorial process, we left the signatures alone to preserve the spirit in which each e-devotion was written.

The Editors

Ann Gelting
Brad Kutrow
Julie Degni Marr
Doug Mays
Melissa Tolmie

Contents

Grace and God's Presence

Years ago a parishioner came to visit me and shared with me that he was having a hard time in his relationship with God. He didn't feel God's presence in his life. What compounded the problem for him was that he had been at a bible study where he had heard a man describe how close he felt to God. As he listened, he experienced a sinking sadness and feeling of inadequacy because he had never had the feelings this man had. He wondered what was wrong with his own faithfulness, and how he could become a more faithful Christian like the man he had heard speak.

But is faith really a feeling? Do we always have to have the overwhelming, ecstatic feeling of God to consider ourselves faithful Christians? Are feelings proof of God's favor?

In my opinion, faith should never be measured by feelings alone. It is nice when we do have a feeling of God's presence. But perhaps we should adjust our expectation about how often we should expect those feelings. Everyday? Probably not. How often, then? I was once told by a monk we should only expect two or three major experiences of God in a lifetime. Now that's adjusting expectations!

Sometimes it's hard to feel God. How can you expect to feel God when you are overwhelmed by work? When you have a headache? When your kids are screaming in the car?

The truth is, feelings come and go. Feelings can be affected by any number of different experiences: the joy of the birth of a child, the loss of a loved one, winning the lottery, drinking a caffeinated drink. Do we feel God sharing His presence during these moments? If not, does it mean He is not with us?

How do we measure our faith? I think trust is the real issue. Do we trust God? Do we trust that He loves us? Do we trust that He will provide for us? Do you trust that He is with you even when we don't notice His presence?

Know that regardless of whether or not you feel God's presence, God is with you during the mundane and mysterious moments of your life. Whether you are driving to work or experiencing a time of personal crisis, God is present. Jesus delights in you. He cares about you.

We are in this together.

Blessings,
Chip

My 11-month-old niece, Madeline, has spent the past month in Hawaii with her parents, whose jobs allow them great flexibility in their schedules. They were so excited about their month there, but Madeline has made Hawaii something less than paradise. She has not comprehended the time change between the East Coast and the middle of the Pacific Ocean. Emails from my stepbrother have most often been dated at 3 or 4 a.m. when he has been up, strolling Madeline around the dark island, wishing they were both asleep. She has finally made the change and they are headed back to the East Coast today!

Toddler time runs on much the same schedule as God's time. I like to be on time for meetings, stick to my daily plan, and keep myself well-organized. When I came to work on Tuesday, three situations arose that blew my schedule apart. It takes getting used to, but after 25 years of parish ministry, I have come to know that the interruptions and the unforeseen events are when God is most present and when I have the best opportunities to be a channel of God's grace.

We should all seek to be organized and timely, but we should also remember the words of Isaiah, "…my thoughts are not your thoughts, nor are your ways my ways, says the Lord. For as the heavens are higher than the earth, so are my ways higher than your ways and my thoughts than your thoughts." The next time your ordered life gets blown apart, look around for God's promptings and/or fingerprints. You may be in the midst of a very holy moment. I'm told that the sounds and smells of Hawaii at 3 or 4 a.m. are sweeter and more peaceful than one could imagine!

Marty

How often have you and I been in situations and said, "Where is God in this? Why am I so alone?" These were the very same questions the disciples asked themselves when the risen Lord left them for a second time and ascended into heaven. Our faith says we are never alone; God is always present with us in some way.

Recently a parish family went through a trying time. Their child was diagnosed with medical problems that require regular, ongoing attention. When the child came back to Christ Church Kindergarten, the parents were concerned about any medical situations arising at school that might cause problems for their child and/or the school. So the parents devised a plan. For the first few days of their child's reentry at school, he would be dropped off as usual. Then the parent would leave the school only to return to the church property and remain on site, but out of sight of the child. One day I saw the dad reading the paper in his car. Another day I saw the mom catching up on some correspondence. The point was that a parent was right by their child in case any need arose, but the child didn't know it, the child didn't see them, and the child carried on **as if he were alone.**

Often God's care is just like that. We may not see God, we may feel alone, but God is present, always ready to give us whatever we need - courage, help, guidance, patience, hope. Whenever you feel God's absence, remember that parish family and take heart. If two parents can be so loving and caring of their child, how much more will our good God and Father in heaven be loving and caring of each of us, his children? Thanks be to God.

The Rev. Martha Hedgpeth

Are you in a rut today? We all get in ruts at some point in our life. It may be a rut in our job or our marriage. It's that feeling that things are just not right. Things seem a little off. We feel unsatisfied.

Scott Peck once wrote "The truth is that our finest moments are most likely to occur when we are feeling deeply uncomfortable, unhappy, or unfulfilled. For it is only in such moments, propelled by our discomfort, that we are likely to step out of our ruts and start searching for different ways or truer answers."

What is going on in your life today? Now that is a big question! Are we willing to face it and deal with it?

Know this: God is much bigger than whatever it is that puts us in a rut. God desires that we live life to the fullest. Irenaeus once wrote, "The joy of God is a human being fully alive."

Breakthroughs always begin with facing the truth. Go there if you can. You'll be glad you did. And you'll find God standing right next to you. He will help you make a new way.

Blessings,
Chip

I have been blessed with three or four conversations in the past few weeks that have reminded me of something that is very important: the beauty and the holiness of each person on this earth. It is a scary thought that I needed to be reminded of something so fundamentally important, but the truth is that it had been much too long since I thought about how beautiful each of us truly is. I had been spending so much time thinking about the present brokenness of the world and of humanity, that I had begun to ignore any possibility of being beautiful or holy in the present.

Is there anyone else out there like me? Is there anyone else who could benefit from spending a little less time these days dwelling on how we are falling short or failing in some way or another? Might it be healthier to spend our time rejoicing in the endless gifts we all possess rather than spending our time fearing we are hopeless in our efforts to do or be enough?

I invite you to join me today as I celebrate each of us right where we are. Join me in remembering that we are each truly beautiful today. Let's claim our holiness and the ways that we have been set apart for special purposes. Celebrate those that are around you today. Seek in yourself and in others the image of God and give thanks for the parts of you and the parts of your neighbors that give light to the world. Give thanks today that Jesus came into the world to save sinners. Realize that he was sent by his Father, who loved the broken of that age, as much as God loves and delights in each one of us here in this age.

John Porter-Acee +

Splangchnizomai. It's a word. I promise. Don't try to pronounce it. But do try to understand its meaning. It can give us a window into the heart and essence of God.

Splangchnizomai is a Greek word found in the Bible that means "to be moved by compassion." It's more than just feeling an emotion. It is the experience of being moved by compassion into action.

At Christmas, we celebrate that God was so splangchnizomai that he came down to love us. As Christians, we believe that he still works among us through the presence of the Holy Spirit. Every now and again we get certain glimpses of His presence. Sometimes it's an awareness that comes to us in a time of need. All of the sudden, unexpectedly, we feel a sense of peace. Other times, Jesus acts through the love of a friend who comes to walk with us through a trial or challenge. In these moments, we have an experience of grace. And life changes.

Splangchnizomai. What a blessing! What hope we have in Jesus. As Henri Nouwen once wrote so beautifully:

"Sshh! Be still. All is well. I am here. Do not be afraid. The world is no longer in the hands of the evil one but in the arms of a loving Shepherd. In the end everything is going to be all right. Nothing can harm you permanently. No suffering is irrevocable, no loss is lasting: no defeat is more than transitory, no disappointment is conclusive. Nothing ever separates us -- not troubles, worries, persecutions, not lack of food or clothes, not attacks or invasions. There is nothing in life or death that will ever come between you and the love of God...."

Thanks be to God for God's compassion and His presence among us. We are in the palm of his gentle hands and he will never let us go. Love and prayers,

Chip

I am a weather geek. It began years ago when I lived on Martha's Vineyard year round and learned how much life for islanders is determined by weather that comes and goes at an alarming pace. I developed a love of tides and fronts and windstreams and such. I love to see how the media covers weather and usually gets it wrong. I love to hear the newscasters freaking out about possible bad weather. I love to see how we tend to treat weather as a product of our making -- we blame the forecasters when it's bad and they take credit when it's good. I love to see the way we act like fools and think the weather cannot deter us -- driving on ice, no matter what vehicle you're in, is just plain stupid!

I love weather because it is such a clear message from God that the created order is not something we can ever fully comprehend or something we can control. Today the forecasters and newscasters are freaking out at the possibility of snow and/or ice tomorrow. Our immediate reaction is to go clear the grocery store shelves of bread and milk. I offer a new way to think of this possible storm. Let's try to see it as a sign of God's majesty and might; a reminder that there are things in life and this world that we cannot control; that we need to be prepared, but even more we need to have the humility to stop and be in awe of something that may bring our lives to a screeching halt for a brief time. It used to be the Sabbath that did that, but no more.

I'm betting that this storm is going to be a non-event, but if it is or it isn't, I'll be on the lookout for signs of God's ongoing presence and power in the atmosphere. And in the event that we do get weather that stops us in our tracks, I suggest you do what I'll do -- read Psalms 104 and 147 and thank God for the beautiful reminder of our place in this beautiful world. Thank God for the modern Sabbath -- weather.

Marty

I was hanging out with some young people the other day. Really young. Julia is two years old; she had a friend over to play, and she was literally squealing with joy. Her brother James, two months old, cooed in my arms and worked hard to produce his first smiles.

Joy seems a rare commodity in the midst of the gloom and doom headlines of late. Is joy tied only to our circumstances? Can we know genuine joy despite and regardless of our situation? True joy is that which rises above our circumstances and is not connected to things or outcomes. For me, there is comfort and hope in knowing success is not a prerequisite for joy. Joy has no need of things in order to bloom. Joy is possible amid failure, disappointment, sickness, and yes, even, death. But when we cannot muster or perceive any joy within us, perhaps we can borrow the joy that God takes in each of us. Nehemiah told the people of Israel, "do not be grieved, for the joy of the Lord is your strength." (Nehemiah 8:10)

Just as Julia and James' parents draw strength from their children's joy, we too can draw strength from the joy of the Lord. God's joy has no limits, no ties to the stock market and is unaffected by the day's headlines. Joy is possible wherever God is present, which means joy is possible anywhere. No matter our circumstances, we too can be a source of joy for others. When we bring others joy, it is hard to keep it from ourselves as well.

John 15:11: I have said these things to you so that my joy may be in you, and that your joy may be complete.
Romans 15:13: May the God of hope fill you with all joy and peace in believing, so that you may abound in hope by the power of the Holy Spirit.
Psalm 16:11: You show me the path of life. In your presence there is fullness of joy; in your right hand are pleasures forevermore.

I trust that joy is in your path today.

Lisa

Every now and again you get a glimpse of something that stops you in your tracks and gives you a new perspective. It happened to me a few weeks ago after a long flight. I will spare you all the details, but there was major turbulence. I was seated directly across from the restroom, and there was a large, snoring man sitting next to me who seemed determined to use my shoulder as a pillow. It was 5½ hours of pure joy.

As the plane stopped at the gate, and I began to walk to the exit in the typical stop-and-go fashion that comes with people taking down their bags and gathering their things, I found myself stopped next to a holy sight that I will not soon forget. There, a few inches from where I stood, was a child, severely handicapped, lying in his mother's lap. In the seat next to them was a portable life support machine, which sent oxygen into his lungs and food into his stomach. I looked briefly at the child, not wanting to appear as though I was staring. I also looked at his young mother, no more than thirty, gently stroking his beautiful, full head of hair.

My guess is that we have all had moments like these when we see something that catches our breath. Interestingly, my own reaction was not pity, but one of genuine respect and curiosity. Lots of questions ran through my head. How did the child get to this state? What did it take to get ready for the trip? How long did it take before they found the courage to travel, in light of the inherent health risks and general hassle? And who was this young woman? Had she always been an extraordinary person? Or was she just an everyday woman who, through unpredictable circumstances, had become a silent hero?

I have known many extraordinary people in my life. None of them would want their lives romanticized. But they remain to me a living testament to what God can do to empower people to meet the challenges they face. One of them once said, "we are called to embrace reality, whatever reality is. And in embracing reality, if we call upon the love and mercy of Jesus, we find a hidden strength to persevere."

Today, with whatever challenge we face, let us do just that. Let us turn to face what we must, knowing, in the words of Psalm 46, "God is our refuge and strength, an ever-present help in trouble. Therefore we will not fear, though the earth give way and the mountains fall into the heart of the sea. The LORD Almighty is with us."

With deep affection,
Chip

In the bookstore this week, a book caught my attention. The title was "A Beautiful Mess." It struck me how well that title describes the human condition. Life can indeed be messy and complicated. Yet when God looks upon us, he sees not just the messes. He sees what at times we cannot see -- the potential in us. I have always believed that God is ultimately a God of love. However, I know that there are many people who for any number of reasons do not know the love of God. And their inability to receive the love of Jesus is actually a wall that blocks them from experiencing God's transforming compassion, tenderness, and presence in life. I've often felt that my ultimate mission as a priest is to convey the unconditional love of God. There have been times that people have asked if I place too much emphasis on God's love. My response has always been I don't think that you can, because God ultimately is love.

As I write it is raining outside. As I look out the window and see the rain saturate the earth I'm reminded of a Peanuts cartoon. Lucy and Linus look out the window at a rainstorm. Lucy says to Linus that she is afraid that the rain might flood the earth. Linus responds by reminding Lucy of God's promise of the rainbow to never flood the earth again. Lucy replies that Linus has made her feel so much better by what he has said. Linus turns to her and says "sound theology has a way of doing that."

C.S. Lewis said that the devil works in half-truths and toxic theology. The half-truth that we fear is that God might love us but He doesn't really accept us as we are. The good theology of the Bible is that God does actually accept us as we are. But He doesn't stop there. God says, "I want to help shape your life. But in order to do that I need for you to trust my love for you. I want you to let me enter more deeply into your heart. I want you to allow me to love you deeply. And as I love you I will help you see how good and capable and beautiful you truly are." This is the whole truth -- the whole truth of God's love for us. Paul Tillich knew this, and wrote, "God's invitation is to accept that we have already been accepted." When we do this, our life with God will take on a wondrous new meaning and depth.

The Rev. Chip Edens

One of my favorite items that I bought and brought home from my time in Jerusalem is a huge decorative egg. They are all over the place in the Holy Land. After seeing them at every turn, I asked one of the locals why they are so prevalent. It turns out that they are fancy replicas of ostrich eggs. It is believed that an ostrich will never venture out of sight of its eggs. And so these fancy replicas are symbols of our relationship with God. Like the ostrich egg, we are never out of God's sight. We may not see God, but God sees us and is ever vigilant over us.

Symbols like this have always helped me. They do not provide some kind of magical shield or protection or automatic answers, but they remind me of the truths of faith that are not quantifiable. They also make mysteries more understandable, tangible, visible images that are imaginative, whimsical, and easy to grasp. The next time you feel the absence of God, think of yourself as an ostrich egg and God as that ostrich parent who always has one eye on you. It very well may strengthen your faith, and it will at least make you smile.

The Rev. Marty Hedgpeth

Christian Living

My mothering and the athletic coaching my daughter receives sometimes are at odds. For instance, I have taught my daughter to look at the bigger picture in the face of disappointments and not to be discouraged by every bump in the road. But apparently, when the team is losing 8-0, coaches frown upon laughter in the dugout.

My daughter plays first base on her high school softball team. When the first base coach for the opposing team was hit hard by a ball, my daughter rushed to his side with compassion and consideration. While I beamed from the bleachers about her good manners, her coach was about to come out of his skin because she did not use the opportunity to tag the runner who stood a foot off the bag, absent-mindedly watching the proceedings.

Then on senior day, when my daughter didn't get to play and was replaced by a senior who ably covered first base, I was proud that my daughter didn't pout or get the least bit upset that she was on the bench the whole game, and was even happy to see her teammate play so well. The coach saw it differently. "I hear you didn't *want* to get in the game yesterday," he said to her the next day, accusingly.

As Verdery likes to tell us, the ball field is rife with life lessons for living out our faith. Jesus frequently stands at odds with the world's coaching. Jesus hung out with losers and told stories that said loss and losing were the only true way to win.

To signify "loser," kids today form their hand into the shape of the letter "L" and place it over their forehead. I was with our 8th grade church school class last Sunday, and one student jokingly said the "L" on his forehead stood for love, not loser. Precisely, Jesus might say. Loving sometimes feels like losing -- not only losing your time, money or talents to tend to someone else's needs -- but losing, even dying, to yourself.

Sunday's reading from 1 John included the word "love" 27 times! Jesus claims that only a life given away for love's sake is a life worth living. It's good to stop and ask yourself every now and then not only which coach are you listening to lately, but also what sort of coaching are you providing for others? My daughter and her softball teammates won over half their games, but I'm proud to say they are also a very fine group of losers.

The Rev. Lisa Saunders

I was ecstatic. Last month at a restaurant in Bay St. Louis, Mississippi, for the first time, being 55, I qualified for a Senior Citizen Discount. I have never been bothered by age -- mine or anyone else's. To borrow an old adage, some of my best friends are old, really old. Older people have taught me the most about the Christian faith -- life, death, joy, sorrow, dignity, courage, patience, humor, and humility.

Recently I saw an amazing documentary called, "Young at Heart." It follows a singing group of senior citizens in Northampton, Massachusetts, who learn "modern music" (Aretha Franklin to Coldplay) and who do concerts in a variety of venues from prisons to Europe. If you want to see how extraordinary older people can be, go see this film. You will laugh and cry and rejoice in the life they reveal.

And having seen that, reach out and get to know some older folks. Last night about 9:30 I sat with my 86-year-old neighbor on her front porch watching the almost full moon. We had some laughs over a crazy neighbor and she updated me on the latest David Letterman jokes -- she watches his show religiously. I went home with a deep sense of peace gained from my neighbor's wise perspective and a deep sense of gratitude that she is a friend. On Saturday I'll be at the birthday party of another friend turning 90! She remains one of the smartest and funniest people I know. When did you last cherish the opportunity to honor and to be friends with a senior citizen? Give older people a little of your time and attention. You'll be amazed at how young they are; you'll be blessed by their wisdom.

The Rev. Marty Hedgpeth

Love is rarely convenient. It is a risky business. There is no way around it. Love requires sacrifice.

Last week our church continued a great 30-year tradition of gathering, wrapping and delivering Christmas presents to low-income families in Duff, Tennessee. It seems like a small task for such a large congregation that is blessed in many ways; but it always has an enormous impact on the families of Duff. Without us, the children of Duff might not know the joy of Christmas. For many of them, these gifts of clothes and a toy are the only items they will receive this year. Over half of the families in Duff live below the poverty level; many have not gone to school beyond eighth grade and about a third of the people in this community do not have running water in their homes or automobiles in their driveways.

Last Wednesday, during one of the busiest times of the year, two of our staff members, Aimee Norman and Van Hill, volunteered to deliver the presents.

I want to emphasize that they volunteered. It was not on-the-clock church work.

They got up very early one morning, drove six hours in an uncomfortable truck along long stretches of highways and poorly maintained mountain roads.

It wasn't convenient for them. They have plenty to do -- trust me. But they knew it needed to be done and they wanted to be the ones to do it. This was their service to Christ in the run up to Christmas.

What will be our risky, inconvenient gift to Christ this Christmas?

Blessings,
Chip

Often when we use the term "thin," it connotes weakness, such as our patience wearing thin, or thinning paint, or judging content to be thin. Celtic spirituality, however, puts a completely different spin on thin.

The Celtics called something thin when the veil between this kingdom and God's kingdom becomes transparent enough for us to glimpse God's presence near us. "Thin places," the Celtics said, are those moments when we can see God's loving hand at work in our life. The sacraments are called thin places. As we gather around the altar at the eucharist each week, we enter a thin place. Today included several sacramental moments for me; I had the privilege of moving from one thin place to another. I celebrated the eucharist, baptized someone, laid hands for healing and anointed with oil someone else. I prayed at the hospital bedside with others. I officiated at the funeral of a loving father and grandfather, and later today I will meet with a couple who are to be married soon. It was an unusually thin day for me, but I love days when I keep bumping into God all day long.

Thin places are not found only at church or just through sacred traditions. Places and moments become thin when someone remembers your pain or offers a helping hand, when words of love arrive unexpectedly, wherever friends share tears or belly shaking laughter. Jesus, of course, was especially thin by Celtic definition. In his life, we see God the most clearly.

In her book, "Walking Through Thin Places," Mindie Borgoyne writes: Thin places are "stopping places where men and women are given pause to wonder about what lies beyond the mundane rituals, the grief, trials and boredom of our day-to-day life. They probe to the core of the human heart and open the pathway that leads to satisfying the familiar hungers and yearnings common to all people on earth, the hunger to be connected, to be a part of something greater, to be loved, to find peace." I hope we meet soon in someplace thin.

Lisa +

The Church Times, the weekly newspaper of the Church of England, is, like the Times of London, famous for its obituaries. Not so long ago, I read the write-up about the Rev. Lawrence Totty, of whom I had never heard but whose stiff-upper-lip faithfulness and doggedness I have to admire. Consider this:

"In 1930, the Bible Churchmen's Missionary Society sent [Totty] to Kacheliba, Kenya, to minister to the Pokot tribe, where he was a pioneer. Conditions were very difficult. He lived in a tent and traveled on donkeys. There was virtually no water in the dry season, and the roads became impassable in the wet season. The Pokot had never heard the gospel, and [Totty] did not speak or understand their language."

Even if I skip the rest of the newspaper, I always skim the obits. How else would I have heard of a man who died at age 94, having translated the New Testament into the Pokot language, about which he had been clueless when he moved to Kenya? How else would I have known that, when he retired after 34 years there, he left behind 12 active churches (built of the bricks he taught himself and his people to make and lighted by electricity he produced by damming a river), 14 schools (ditto), and many Christians, one of whom has been ordained a bishop?

Then I encountered Kathleen Norris' book, "The Quotidian Mysteries": "In our life of faith, as well as in our most intimate relationships with other people, our task is to transform the high romance of conversion, the fervor of a religious call, into daily commitment, into the sort of friendship that transcends infatuation and can endure all things. Our desire is to love God and each other, in stable relationships that, like any good marriage, remain open to surprises and receptive to grace."

Kathleen Norris, meet Lawrence Totty. My hunch is that Totty, while learning Pokot and making bricks and damming rivers, moved from the fervor that took him to Kenya in the first place into a life of enduring all things and of daily commitment, full of surprises and transfused by grace. By such daily-ness does God do some of God's best work. By our slogging on does God bring us along.

I don't know that I have ever been in any of Totty's churches, but I have been to brick churches in Kenya, including two in the upland coffee-growing area that could have been transplanted from the Cotswolds. I have worshipped alongside people who sang in what could well have been Pokot Victorian hymns with a fervor and a beauty you can't imagine. I have heard "Stand up, stand up for Jesus" and "Onward Christian Soldiers" rendered with intensity and harmonies that must make the angels weep for joy. And maybe that happened in one of the brick churches built by a man who went to Kenya to people who had no notion why he was there and with whom he couldn't communicate.

Perhaps together they learned to "remain open to surprises and receptive to grace." Certainly they must have taught each other about the holy movement from the initial enthusiasm of being changed to being those who live their lives on the basis of a workaday commitment to each other and to the God who brought them together.

And perhaps, too, there is a model here for our life together at Christ Church. Call it the "Totty model." It might go something like this: A miscellany of people of good will gather in a self-selected group on the basis of the enthusiasm each brings, finding as they live together that their initial enthusiasms are being transfused by surprises and grace to the point where they discover why it was that they came together in the first place --which, in Kathleen Norris' words, has something to do with loving God and loving each other. Like Father Totty, we may be initially clueless about what we are up to, but gradually and by God's grace, we discover our own workaday commitment to each other and to the God of surprises who brings us together and keeps us where we may grow and bloom.

The Rev. Nick White

A couple of weeks ago, I preached about the heart of Christianity as doing faith rather than having faith. It was interesting to have so many people respond afterward in a way that implied, "I really want to do something, but I feel nothing I do really makes a difference." Of course, if we could bring about world peace, we would do it; if we could end hunger, we would do it. But God doesn't ask us to do such big things. God asks us to do little things.

I recently read an article by Samuel Wells that talked about this. He described French villagers in World War II who took in Jewish escapees from central Europe. They gave them hospitality for a few days and then sent them on their way to Switzerland. Wells writes, "The point was not that such actions would end the Holocaust or win the war; the gestures demonstrated the self-giving love of God revealed in Christ and offered a foretaste of the fellowship to be perfected in heaven."

How often has a little gesture offered by someone brightened a moment or a day for you or even saved your life? It happens for me often, and I am so grateful for those gestures. Maybe we should attempt faith gestures, little acts, that may not change the world, but may change a moment of life for someone in a way that points to God's ultimate changing of the whole world.

The Rev. Marty Hedgpeth

I hadn't thought of Mrs. Viallon in years. But in Costa Rica on the Christ Church "One In the Spirit" mission trip a few weeks ago, Mrs. Viallon was on my mind a lot. She was my high school Spanish teacher. I was channeling Mrs. Viallon's spirit and vocabulary quizzes quite a bit while in San Jose, and was remarkably surprised at how much I remembered nearly three decades later. Mrs. Viallon would have been so proud.

Ironically, one phrase I particularly remember from Mrs. Viallon's class is the following: *En la boca cerrada no entran las moscas.* Mrs. Viallon used to say this as a reminder to her students to keep quiet in class. The phrase is the equivalent of "A closed mouth catches no flies." Our Costa Rican friends laughed when I spouted Mrs. Viallon's admonition to her students. Apparently it is not a Spanish saying but the Spanish equivalent of an English adage.

We did learn a Spanish saying, one that is particular to Costa Rica and something of a national slogan. "*La pura vida,*" Costa Ricans say this to each other as a means to express wellness and goodness. Literally, it translates "the pure life." Yet I would liken the use of "*pura vida*" in Costa Rica to the use of the word "cool" in America. For example, How are you? *Pura vida.* That boy is very *pura vida.* How was the prom? *Pura vida*, Mom. "*Pura vida*" also doubles as "good luck" in Costa Rica, and I imagine that in a Star Wars movie dubbed in Spanish, the phrase "the force be with you" could be replaced with "*la pura vida*" and nothing missed in the translation.

I love the phrase "*pura vida,*" because the pure life was much of what I experienced in Costa Rica and a sense of which I hope I brought home with me. The pure life can be found when we learn to stop passing judgment on others and open ourselves to trusting that each person has something to teach us. The pure life begins when we spend time doing work that seeks only to widen the grace of someone else's life. The pure life is unveiled with the bonds of warm friendships made by praying, working, dancing, laughing, and crying together. The pure life cuts deep when we are stopped short by the enchanting beauty of God's creation (try standing in a garden with the sights and sounds of a hundred hummingbirds of all different colors and sizes flying around you). The pure life enters in when we experience the holy, the sacred, God's Spirit in our midst. For me *la pura vida* could be translated *the Kingdom of God.* I was glad for all the Spanish I remembered from Mrs. Viallon's class but blessed by the Spanish I learned anew.

The Rev. Lisa Saunders

There is something entirely glorious about saying "I'm sorry." At times it is hard to do. And yet a real, heart felt apology is the very best thing to help move relationships forward.

What makes such denial so dangerous? When we deny the realities and repercussions of mistakes we have made, we run the risk of alienating people and damaging relationships we need.

As followers of Christ, we must always commit to being lovers of truth. We must not run from our mistakes. Sometimes it is painful to examine the truth. However, the hope for progress in all matters of life, from politics, to addiction, to marriage, lies in our ability to come to terms with truth, to repent, to accept God's forgiveness, and to extend it to others.

In the end, God can heal us and help us grow into more compassionate people. And in that moment of reconciliation when someone says, "I forgive you," we can begin to feel our relationship being restored; we can understand the joy in being wrong.

Blessings,
Chip

I see that the Roman Catholic Church has launched an ad campaign to encourage married couples in their life together. The ads emphasize the importance of small kindnesses and the website (Foryourmarriage.org) stresses the fact that everyone loses that loving feeling at one time or another. Sometimes it is the commitment of marriage alone that helps a couple span a difficult patch.

When a couple marries, they cannot imagine that promising to be faithful for better, for worse, in sickness and in health, 'til death do us part, could ever be anything but a walk in the park. We all know situations where marriages cannot, and even should not, survive despite the promises made and earnest, prayerful efforts to restore the marriage to life-giving form. We lean instead on God's promises of forgiveness, resurrection, hope and healing.

Most governments support the institution of marriage not necessarily for any religious reason, but because good marriages create good citizens. Marriages that work draw out the best from the people in them. There may not be anything more beautiful than witnessing two people honor their vows to cherish, honor and love one another in the midst of illness, tragedy, parenting, grief and challenges of aging. Sometimes love does not sustain the marriage, but marriage sustains the love. I don't think it is within any one of us to keep the vows made at a marriage altar, and that is why couples need to go to the altar: to invite, and to keep inviting, God's grace and love into their marriage so that the life of each has a fighting chance of being blessed and enriched by having the other in it.

Lisa+

Tertullian, a 3rd century Christian renowned for his writings, teaching and preaching on the Christian faith, once quoted a non-Christian writer saying, "See how these Christians love one another." Apparently the behavior of some Christians then was remarkable enough to have been noted by an outsider. I was reminded of this statement a couple of weeks ago at our monthly breakfast for men dubbed First Fridays for Men. At this meal it has been customary for the speaker to address a topic pertaining to a challenge of following Jesus in the contemporary world. A recent speaker, a parishioner, spoke of the link between epidemics and key transitional moments in the Bible. He offered a theory about the spread of Christianity I find compelling. Rather than superb teaching, preaching and worship as primary factors for the expansion of the faith in early centuries, a chief influence was the consistent capacity of Christians to care for the sick, injured and dying. During epidemics and war when the prevailing behavior was to keep unhealthy, damaged people at a distance, Christians did just the opposite. They went to places of sickness and pain others avoided. Cumulatively these efforts of care and courage began to have a significant impact. They drew hundreds to conversion.

We've all heard the advice, "The best sermon is not the one preached. It's the one lived." Fred Paschal, parishioner and former associate, regularly quotes Francis of Assisi, "Preach the Gospel always. Use words if necessary." What I heard at First Friday for Men was that the lived Gospel was inspiration for the growth of Christianity. The examples we set and those set for us are formidable. They are essential determinants more so than spoken words. It's the doing which makes the difference.

In Christ,
Verdery

And he was with the wild beasts ... (Mark 1:13).

I have known only one actual wild beast. Nelson, my Jack Russell terrier, has now retired to a farm in Mississippi. Before leaving the Queen City, though, he blazed a trail of destruction that still has people talking. I once visited a friend who was in the hospital recovering from abdominal surgery. She said that her operation had been relatively painless, frankly, compared to those occasions when she had helped me walk my dog. Nelson was fond of eating tennis shoes, parading around in women's lingerie, and pulling his handlers right off their feet. I will love him until the day I die, though things around my house are much easier without him.

When I think about the sorts of "wild beasts" that are in my life these days, I tend to think not of animals but of those things about myself and about our world that feel out of control, things that I would like to tame: an overcrowded schedule; my self-centeredness; my tendency to be judgmental of others; worries about violence and terrorism; anxiety about a loved one's health. Through the years, I have prayed many times that God would remove these beasts from my life, that I would become more the loving, trusting, peaceful person God calls me to be and that our world would come to reflect more fully God's intentions for it. By God's grace, I have seen progress in some areas. Slowly, but surely, our world, and all of us who inhabit it, are being changed. Some of my inner beasts, however, seem destined to be like St. Paul's infamous "thorn in the flesh." Pray though I might, I suspect they will always be with me in one form or another.

Maybe this is why I find the classic Lenten text of Mark 1:12-13 so comforting. In it, we read that Jesus, during his forty days in the wilderness, lived among wild beasts. Mark doesn't give us many details about this. We know only that Jesus and the wild beasts co-existed and that God gave his Son the will to persevere. He did not take the wild beasts away; neither did he let Jesus be overcome by them.

Chaos, imperfection, danger, sickness and sin will always be part of our lives this side of the grave. With God as our helper, though, we can learn to co-exist with these forces and not let them rule us or drive us to despair. Through prayer and perseverance, we can be strengthened to bear our crosses just as Christ was strengthened to bear his. We can learn to live with our wild beasts. Occasionally, we can even make some of them our friends.

The Rev. Julia Boyd

This past weekend Beverly and I went away to the mountains for a time of relaxation and restoration. We needed time for rest as well as time to restore aspects of our life together. Life as a couple too easily gets pushed aside by the daily demands and unexpected emergencies that accompany a family with three small children and life in an energetic and demanding Church.

Over the course of the weekend we enjoyed many things: the red, gold, and yellow leaves, walks by a swollen river, the moonlight reflecting on a lake, the wind in the trees, and the crack and pop of a roaring fire. We also had a chance to finish conversations we had started as well as begin new ones about the future. Most especially, we had the privilege of resting.

Now that we are home, I find myself thinking of the ancient directive of God to honor the Sabbath. Time set apart for restoration is an essential part of life. We may think we can put rest off -- or even that we may not need to rest at all. Yet, this act of neglecting our need for renewal and healing will always come back to haunt us.

During this busy time of year, it is such a blessed feeling to have the energy to finish what I need to do. I haven't always felt this way. I have had to learn this lesson the hard way, causing damage to my health and family by working too much. I realize now how important the Sabbath time is to one's overall well-being. I also realize that God gave it to us for a reason: that we might have life "and have it abundantly."

How are you doing with your Sabbath time? When is your next time away? Do you have anything scheduled on your calendar, even if it is just a day alone, or an afternoon with someone you love? What in your life needs to be healed and restored?

With love and prayers,
Chip

"Nobody likes to be told what to do." That's the chapter heading in a little book I was reading. The words jumped out at me because I am the queen of telling people what to do. My savvy husband has learned simply to go on and do what he wants despite my brilliant ideas. It frightens me to think about how much of the conversation between me and my children consists of direction and criticism. My oldest child has gotten very good at pointing this out to me with comments like, "This is no longer a conversation; this has become a lecture." Or "How is what you are saying helpful to me?"

Most of us don't like to be told what to do, yet we usually ask God for direction and guidance in our lives. In fact, sometimes we are disappointed or frustrated because God isn't more direct with us. And yet the times Jesus did get specific, folks wound up wishing they hadn't asked in the first place. To the one who asked, "who is my neighbor?" Jesus said your neighbor is a stranger, with multiple needs, requiring immediate and great sacrifice from you.

Oh.

To Peter, who bragged at forgiving someone as many as seven times, and asked if he could stop, Jesus said, "No, Peter. I do not ask you to forgive seven times, but seventy times seven times."

Oh.

As Mark Twain said, "It ain't the parts of the Bible that I can't understand that bother me, it's the parts that I do understand."

Jesus sets the bar high for us. Most of us like to set the bar high for our children, but they cannot be lectured or criticized into clearing it. What encourages me to follow God's leading is not fear of what will happen if I don't, but the impression that God cares more about me than about whether I can make the right choices or not. God promises that no matter what we do, God will not leave us, and that there is always hope for healing, for peace, for reconciliation, for starting over, for deep, fulfilling joy. As much as I love to tell people what to do, Jesus' idea is better. I'd much rather be someone who gives people hope than direction.

Lisa

I cleaned out my office last week. Interestingly, everyone who witnessed that had the exact same reaction. Over and over I was asked, "Are you going somewhere?" It was as if the only legitimate reason to clear out a bunch of stuff is in order to vacate the space! I have no plans to go anywhere, but I like to clean out my home and my office regularly. It is an act both fun and faithful. First, there is the wonderful walk down memory lane as I come across items that were gifts from all sorts and conditions of people. Second there is the discovery of items I thought had been lost. Third, there is a real sense of unburdening and freedom that comes with getting rid of stuff that is not being used. Fourth, there is a chance to examine and reorder my priorities.

When Jesus sent the disciples out to do ministry, "He ordered them to take nothing for their journey except a staff; no bread, no bag, no money in their belts; but to wear sandals and not to put on two tunics." While the specifics of our lives may be very different from those first disciples, the point is clear: Travel light. In a world gone mad with accumulating unnecessary things, the challenge of Jesus is to let go of all the stuff, see how very little we really need, and discover how very much God gives. Whether you're going somewhere or not, what's piling up in your drawers and closets? Try clearing out a bit and you will be amazed at what you receive in the process.

Marty

I remember watching Neil Armstrong take the first steps on the moon. I was at my aunt and uncle's cabin on Lake Wylie. The moon walk was delayed and didn't actually occur until well after my and my cousins' bedtime, but our parents awakened us to watch the historic event. Now the Phoenix unmanned spacecraft has landed on Mars and is sending back photographs and eventually information that will help NASA's long term goals which include determining whether life ever arose on Mars, characterizing Mars' climate and geology and preparing for human exploration.

I am reminded of a definition of faith that I like: **Faith is the courage to act as if we are not cosmically alone.** This definition keeps me from downsizing God and underestimating God's power to care for me in my own small corner of the world. It helps me send my children off into far corners of the world, too, knowing that they are never beyond God's grace and outstretched hand.

When we act as if we are not cosmically alone, we trust that despite everything that frightens us, exhausts us, frustrates us, mystifies us, angers us, and demoralizes us, we have access to the power that not only sets the stars in the skies but can make all things new. Often courage is doing what you have to do and being surprised that it looks like courage to someone else.

I think part of why we keep wondering if there is life on other planets stems from a deep desire to know we are not alone in the universe. Whatever challenge your universe holds for you right now, I hope this devotion serves as a reminder that God accompanies you with love to sustain and encourage you.

Lisa +

I often come to Christ Church when there are few or no others around -- sometimes early in the day, less often late at night. (Frankly, it's hard to be here when the place is not alive with activity.) As energizing as it is to be here when the place is full and buzzing, it's also good to experience the fullness of the empty space.

Then it's full of the shadows of those who have been here before us, filled with the dreams, hopes, fears, sadnesses they in their time brought to their parish church, just as we do now, filling every cranny with the mist of what makes life holy and full.

I am drawn to the nave, to the church itself, when it seems to be empty, for then am I so aware of the cumulative experience of the times I have entered that sacred space, especially 30 years ago when I served here. I experience in a complicated harmony the weddings, funerals, baptisms, and all the other services simple and grand that have marked this holy space's history as where so many people have gathered to say their prayers since it was built five decades ago.

When the church is empty and quiet, I think of T. S. Eliot's words in "Little Gidding":

"You are not here to verify,
instruct yourself, or inform curiosity
or carry report.
You are here to kneel
where prayer has been valid."

And then I think of the generations of prayers and pray-ers that this holy space has sheltered, the unnumbered acts of trusting faith or of spiritual need seeking faith that have hummed and bounced around in that sacred room. Prayers of thanksgiving, of deep, deep need, of unspeakable joy or hope or sorrow -- all these prayers have been valid here because they have signaled hearts open to the transforming love of God.

And I give thanks that there is such a place for me now. May it be so for you. May we always enter it in the knowledge that we are walking on holy ground, made holy by the faith and faithfulness of those who have been here before us as well as of those with whom we share it now.

The Rev. Nick White

My daughter will be 18 in a few days, which is amazing, since I was 18 only a few years ago myself. Or so it seems. As I reflect on my hopes for this adult daughter of mine, the words of our liturgies in the church keep coming to mind.

"You are sealed by the Holy Spirit in baptism and marked as Christ's own forever." Henry Parsley said these words as he thumbed the sign of the cross on her infant forehead. Eighteen years in our home is not forever, and while it seems that there has never been a time she has not been part of me, the years have gone like the proverbial blink of an eye. I am comforted that she belongs to someone forever, and that that someone loves her perfectly and completely and unendingly as I might have hoped I could.

"Strengthen you in all goodness..." These words are said after we confess our sins each week. There is much in the world that can weaken and fragment us, maybe even especially for a young woman. We may be made tougher and stronger by our mistakes, failures and disappointments, but I have more trust in the forces of goodness to strengthen her for life's work.

"Empower her for your service..." Bishop Gary Gloster said as he laid his hands upon her teenage head at confirmation. She is being asked these days what she wants to be when she grows up, what does she want to major in at college, what are her goals and plans. She knows more about what she doesn't want to do than what she wants to do. Whatever it develops and reveals itself to be for her, I hope she recognizes that serving Christ can happen, and give life its deepest meaning, anywhere.

"In your infinite love, you made us for yourself." We hear these words as part of the Eucharistic Great Thanksgiving. I sometimes think my daughter was made just for me, but I know that she is really God's glory.

"Send us out to do the work you have given us to do" we pray at the close of the Eucharist service. It was the plan from the moment she was born that one day she would leave us. For Tim and me, she is the work given to us; and we will send her forth, knowing God has work for her to do, and confident that such work can bring her the joy we have known in ours.

For Jews, the number eighteen and the word for "life" use the same Hebrew letters, and so "18" is considered a lucky number. So be it, my daughter, so be it.

The Rev. Lisa Saunders

Recently I was watching some children on a playground, and as so often happens, eventually one little boy was teased and roughed up a bit by the others. The parents of the taunted child were present, and it was painful to see the hurt and anger in their faces; but being seasoned parents, they did not intervene. Eventually their son stood his ground, and the other kids backed off. And within minutes the ostracized boy was once again one of the group.

I think all of us have had experiences being the teased child, one of the teasers, or the parent in that scene. It reminds me of a great line from "The Kite Runner" where a father says, "A boy who won't stand up for himself becomes a man who can't stand up to anything." It is a very important aspect not only of daily life, but also the life of faith.

Far too often we Christians let others rough us up, and we do nothing. Or we allow other Christians to say and do things that we find contrary to the Gospel (such as the theology of prosperity or the notion that America is God's chosen nation). Standing up for our faith isn't about being exclusionary or boastful or rude; it is about making the good news known simply and clearly and joyfully. The next time you have an opportunity to witness to the Gospel, remember that God our Father is watching us and is counting on us to stand up for Jesus.

The Rev. Marty Hedgpeth

A month ago with members of the Koinonia Farms community near Americus, Georgia, I attended Sunday School and a worship service at a Baptist Church in Plains, Georgia, where former President Carter is a member. The draw that morning was the Sunday School class led by President Carter. He is in charge of the adult class twice a month. Secret Service men and women were in abundance, assessing and checking the several hundred people who came that day to hear him. The audience hailed from throughout the United States and countries beyond. The congregation itself numbers less than 150. I was told that they do not resent the surge of visitors when President Carter speaks, which presents parking problems, long lines and scarce seats. They see this as an opportunity for visitors who know little if anything of Scripture to have passages of the Bible presented to them.

When the class concluded, most, including our Koinonia delegation, remained for the service that followed. I noted in the bulletin that the text the Southern Baptist pastor had chosen for the sermon centered on the verse John 14:6: "No one comes to the Father except through me." Knowing that in recent years the Southern Baptist Convention leadership has been unwaveringly literal in its interpretation of this verse, I wondered what the preacher would say. I expected that he would apply it to the present in a distinctly exclusive manner, crafting the meaning to be just as the words sound. To my amazement, he devoted the entire sermon to a refutation of this one-dimensional understanding of the verse. He cited numerous instances where an exclusive interpretation prompted and fed horrific abuses of human beings. I heard an approach to Scripture far from what I expected. He denounced the easy tendency to absolutize a verse or passage without respect for the time and place where it arose. Context matters greatly, he claimed. The situation which Jesus and John addressed was internal. Followers of Jesus and members of the early Church were contending with sabotage from within. There were break-offs inside, purporting to improve what Jesus had begun. The words are for the already converted, not those on the outside.

It was a most interesting sermon...a surprise to hear from a Southern Baptist pulpit rather than say, an Episcopal one. I was reminded that things are not always as expected nor as they appear. In Plains, there is more than one way to understand and apply John 14:6.

The Rev. Verdery Kerr

A playwright. A banker. A lawyer. A homemaker. An artist. A NASA physicist. And two ministers. Eight of us gathered at a small Indian restaurant. Most of us had been in school together since third grade, but nearly thirty years have passed since some of us have laid eyes on each other. There was a lot of "remember when...?" conversation, laughing at old pictures and catching up on news.

It's always fascinating to see how gifts, characteristics and traits present in even third grade find direction, purpose and blossom into an adult's life work and vocation. Certainly each one of us made choices that opened and shut doors all along the way, yet what lay deep inside our scrub-faced, third grade self is still what largely defines who we are today.

Scripture says God knows the number of hairs on our head, and now we do know that a strand of hair can identify us and differentiate us from every other creature on the earth. As many in our congregation celebrate graduations and other milestones that lead them to new endeavors and opportunities, I am reminded that each one of us from birth has been given a unique set of gifts and abilities and passions for the building up of God's kingdom. As Paul writes in Ephesians, God's "gifts were...to equip the saints for the work of ministry, for building up the body of Christ, until we all attain...the measure of the stature of the fullness of Christ... We are to grow up in every way into him who is the head, into Christ, from whom the whole body, joined and knit together by every joint with which it is supplied, when each part is working properly, makes bodily growth and upbuilds itself in love." (Eph. 4:11-16)

To grow up is to know and utilize your gifts for the good of all creation, and those gifts are already intrinsically ours. We can and must learn skills to make and pay our way through life, but we are created with gifts that enrich and energize our careers, our relationships, and, yes, even our souls.

Those of us at dinner the other night are all grown up, but it was oh-so-fun to be with people who remember our third grade self and know that, in many ways, we have not changed at all. "For you yourself created my inmost parts; you knit me together in my mother's womb. I will thank you because I am marvelously made; your works are wonderful, and I know it well." (Psalm 139:12-13)

The Rev. Lisa Saunders

We have a small garden in our backyard. It is sorely neglected, covered in weeds, and yet still yields some fruit. Last week I harvested 12 green beans -- just enough to put on the table for my husband and me one night. The tomatoes are small but, again, enough for our family to enjoy.

Yesterday I went to the garden of parishioner Frank Horne, Sr. His is a beautiful garden, with tomato plants eight feet tall. His rows of vegetable plants are meticulous and well-weeded, and the vegetables produced are plump, juicy and plentiful. He has more than enough to share with others, which he does with great joy and delight. He reminds me of a friend in a farming town in Montana who says that if you don't lock your car during the summer, you'll return and find it filled with zucchini. Gardens there are teeming with produce that folks need to give away.

Jesus frequently made farming metaphors when talking about spiritual matters. The lesson I learn from the difference between my garden and Mr. Horne's is that it is too easy to become satisfied with spiritual lives that require little effort and yield meager fruit. So what if the fruit is small, as long as there is still fruit? What is so important about intentional and daily tending and fertilizing and weeding of the gardens of our faith? The difference is that neglected gardens like mine are selfish gardens and feed only myself, and then only inadequately. Jesus needs followers (and gardeners) who realize that part of why we nurture our faith is so we can bear fruit for others to enjoy and to be fed and nourished. When Jesus spoke of the growth of the tiny mustard seed, he concluded by saying the plant "puts forth large branches, so that the birds of the air can make nests in its shade." Our faith is more than just about and for ourselves, and meant to extend beyond our own backyards.

The Rev. Lisa Saunders

Last week while doing some research, I discovered this quote by N. T. Wright, a renowned New Testament scholar from England: "There is such a thing as evil, and it is to be addressed and defeated not by ignoring it on the one hand or by blasting away at it with heavy artillery on the other...but by addressing it with the message and methods of the cross."

When we encounter something which is hard, unjust, painful, ugly, corrupt, nasty, perhaps subtle and masked, etc., in our repertoire of responses is the popular one of making it go away. We make "it" go away by denying or pretending an evil isn't present. We make "it" go away by going unconscious and choosing not to see the darkness. Many are the times individual and corporate abuse or exploitation is sustained by such blindness. We make "it" go away too by lashing out and countering an evil with force: vanquishing, obliterating, conquering, exterminating. A big win over evil brings short-term comfort; creates an illusion, short-circuits pain for the meantime.

I am reminded of a statement from an amazing 20th century mystic, Howard Thurman: "Nobody ever wins a fight."... which is to say that the defeated forever desire payback, retribution, to settle the score...and the cycle of winning and losing persists over generations, regions and nations...and even over centuries. It doesn't require much knowledge of world history to know this to be a deep pattern.

I see in Jesus an uncommon way of contending with evil. He neither acted as if it didn't exist nor did he opt to crush it. He repeatedly called it out, engaged it, did not flinch and did not try to "bomb" it into submission. Getting evil off our radar screens is so much easier than what Jesus did. It requires stunning poise, strength, self-discipline, courage to "stand-up" to evil as he did. A few verses from 1 Corinthians underscore why there is only one Jesus: "For God's foolishness is wiser than human wisdom, and God's weakness is stronger than human strength... God chose what is foolish in the world to shame the wise; God chose what is weak in the world to shame the strong; God chose what is low and despised in the world, things that are not, to reduce to nothing things that are..."

Part of being Easter people is living this uncommon way.

Verdery

The Sunday morning services were over; the pews had emptied out. Prayers, praise, hymns and gifts had all been offered up to God, yet one of the most important offerings had yet to be given. On a Sunday this past August, parishioner Gilbert Browne was assisting his wife, Jane, with Altar Guild duties when a little girl walked up the center aisle of the church. Gilbert wrote to me of his encounter with the child and included an enclosure with his note. I'll let Gilbert tell the story from here:

I was standing behind the altar, clad in white gloves and wrestling with the candles to prepare them for the next service. This little person who was no older than four, looked me in the eye seriously as she approached the altar and softly said, "Please, give this to God." (Her offering to God is enclosed.) She then trotted down the center aisle and out of the church. Needless to say, I was dumbstruck as the enclosed is a holy document. Inside Gilbert's note was a small page from a coloring book. The picture was colored with crayons as a four-year-old might do, and at the bottom of the page was written:
To: God
♥ Grace

Gilbert wrote further:

Throughout the day since then, I have been thinking about what I give to God and what I really need to give to God. I am thankful that little Grace, a precious child of God, has set my mind that way this day, and hopefully, for many days to come.

Grace also prompts me to think about what I will give to God today. What prayers and acts of mercy, generosity, self-denial, and kindness will we hand over to God today? We may not deliver our holy offering to the altar as little Grace did, but I have no doubt that, like her gift, our gift today will delight God and will be used to increase hope, healing and an awareness of God's blessings around us.

Lisa+

What do you do when people offend you? Let's admit it: people do constantly offend us. How could they act that way? People that we love hurt us: our spouses, our children, and our friends. Their words and actions hurt the most. They are supposed to love us after all!

Many of us carry around these deep-seated resentments. Are we aware of what the hurt is doing to us? Consider these words from Frederick Buechner: "Of the Seven Deadly Sins, anger is possibly the most fun. To lick your wounds, to smack your lips over grievances long past, to roll over your tongue the prospect of bitter confrontations still to come, to savor to the last toothsome morsel both the pain you are given and the pain you are giving back -- in many ways it is a feast fit for a king. The chief drawback is that what you are wolfing down is yourself. The skeleton at the feast is you."

What a startling thought, that due to a lack of forgiveness, we are the ones who hurt the most. It is true. Our inability to forgive holds us in a prison that steals our emotional and spiritual energy. This energy could otherwise be used and redirected towards having deep and satisfying relationships.

Jesus was once asked, "How many times must I forgive?" The people wanted to know what the number of times was before they could write someone off. Jesus gave them an answer in which He explained that forgiveness was not just an act but a way of life they were called to live for the rest of their lives.

May we recommit ourselves to the ongoing work of forgiveness as a way of life so that we might not only release others from their offenses but so that we might also be freed up to live and love and begin again.

With love and prayers,
The Rev. Chip Edens

My nephew starts law school this fall in a town where he knows no one and has met only one person in his class. He was musing about the random encounters one has that often result in lasting friendships. Will it be the neighbor on the other side of his duplex, or something more random and circuitous like the cousin of a friend of a study partner? My nephew realizes that soon he will meet people who will be key figures and support in his journey -- and he for them. For now, they are still strangers, and how their paths will cross is still unknown; and yet already they are headed in a direction that will intersect and then intertwine.

Our world is full of random events and encounters, both wonderful and horrific, and some might see that as evidence to prove God is not in control or all powerful. Has everything that happens to us and to those we love been ordained and orchestrated by God? Does God choose who gets sick and who wins the lottery? Cambridge physicist and priest John Polkinghorne has wondered about these same questions. He writes that "we should understand these widespread unpredictabilities, not as meaning that the world is somehow meaninglessly random, but that it is open to other kinds of causes in addition to those described by physics alone. I think that is how we act in the world. I think that is how God acts in world history, too."

In other words, what we do matters. I believe it is God who has chosen to create a world in which this is the case. The world is not closed or fixed, but as Polkinghorne says, "supple and subtle." Tragedies like global warming, oil spills, drunk driving deaths, war and terrorism are the result of human choices intersecting with the natural order of this world. And so are medical cures, peaceful resolutions, forgiveness, kindness, sacrifice, and courageous perseverance in the face of adversity. Possibilities for goodness and justice are not fixed but endlessly open and subject not only to our choices, but also to God's healing presence and persistent call to discipleship.

My nephew wonders what serendipitous story will accompany his meeting new and dear friends this year, and I have no doubt such stories will emerge. But I also hope he takes his father's advice, and when his neighbor in the duplex arrives this week, he's out on the sidewalk helping her move in.

The Rev. Lisa Saunders

"My aunt is dying," the woman said. "Could you please bring her communion? I've been trying for weeks to find an Episcopal priest who will come." Ordinarily I am glad to bring communion to folks. In this case, neither the aunt nor the niece is a member of Christ Church, and the aunt lives in a nursing home in Indian Trail. It was late Thursday afternoon. I grumbled to myself, but I got a communion kit and headed out Idlewild Road. If you stay on Idlewild long enough, you pass a Buddhist Temple and a llama ranch. On my way to the nursing home, I drove through the little town of Hemby Bridge and passed Fred Kirby Park (I think you have to be at least 50 and have grown up in North Carolina to know who Fred Kirby is).

It took me forty minutes to get to the nursing home in Lake Side, which turned out to be one of the nicest nursing homes I have ever been in. Mrs. P. was in the last room down a long hallway, lying on her side in the bed by the window. Her eyes opened when I said her name. I pulled a chair up close to the bed, told her who I was and that I had brought communion. As we talked, I was enchanted by her and by her story. She was the oldest of 14 children growing up in Massachusetts. She went to school to become a mechanic, joined the Navy and was stationed in Brunswick, Maine during World War II repairing airplanes. "But my whole life, I never rode in a plane," she said. She met her husband, a Marine, during the war; they married months after meeting, before he went back to the Pacific. "I was married 61 and a half years," she said, and the way she added that half-year made it sound like she counted every day with him as precious. "I'm old and tired and ready to die," she said. "Are you afraid at all?" I asked. "There's nothing to be afraid of. The next life is going to be far more wonderful than this one."

After a while I began to set up communion. "When was the last time you had communion?" I asked. "Yesterday," she replied. I froze. "Yesterday? But your niece said..." Turns out someone at the nursing home arranged for communion to be brought to her, and her niece didn't know it.

I could just see God chuckling. I drove out to Indian Trail not because I had something to offer Mrs. P. but because she had something to give me.

Lisa

"Come Labor On," written by Jane Laurie Borthwick, is my second favorite hymn. We sang it Sunday in church and the theme of the third verse seemed to remain a theme for my week.

The third verse reads:

"Come, labor on. Away with gloomy doubts and faithless fear! No arm so weak but may do service here: by feeblest agents may our God fulfill his righteous will."

In a society that often makes people feel like they are measured by their career or their position, it is important to remember that God sees us all as equals. God delights more in the widow's mite than he does in the gold and silver that is not given sacrificially. (Mark 12:41-44). God also delights in the child that writes letters to shut-ins, the shut-ins that stuff envelopes for their church mailings, the mothers that lovingly care for their children, and the teens that speak hesitantly about their faith with a friend that is going through a tough time.

No matter who we are, or where we are, we always have the opportunity to be a delight to God and join in doing the labor of the Lord. Each of us has the gifts and the strength that we need to be a blessing to others. Each of us can play a role in manifesting God's love to the world. Each of us has the opportunity in our life to hear the words that God speaks at the end of Borthwick's wonderful hymn, "Servants, well done."

John Porter-Acee +

Tim and I moved to Charlotte 22 years ago today. It was blazing hot that day, and the air-conditioner in our just-purchased home did not turn on. Apparently we bought a house with an air-conditioner that worked right up until the day we moved in. On our first day as homeowners, we had to buy a brand new air conditioner.

Our realtor recommended the name of a small heating and air company to help us. Norman, the company owner, took one look at me (seven months pregnant), and stayed at our house until 10:00 p.m. installing a new air conditioner. Norman said he couldn't stand for us to have a bad impression of Charlotte on our first day in town. Norman sweated in the heat all day, determined to get us cool air before we went to bed that night. As he watched Norman, my husband Tim, said he was reminded that he would rather see a sermon than hear one any day. I opted to ignore the possible commentary my husband could be making about all the sermons he has had to listen to, and agreed that Norman had "preached" a very fine sermon to us that day.

When I wrote Norman a check at the end of the day, I asked the name of his company. "His Way Heating and Air," he said. A little more conversation, and I learned that Norman, a devout Christian, named his company such because he intended to run his business His way.

I think about Norman today not just because it's hot and my house is cool, but more so because he reminds me that being a disciple of Jesus Christ is not only about prayer and worship and reading the bible. It's also about living and working His way. If it's possible to install an air-conditioner His way over other ways, it's possible to do the laundry His way, take a deposition His way, call on a customer His way, mow the lawn His way, speak to a waiter His way. Of course, we'd all rather see a sermon than hear one, and every now and then let's hope we might actually be the sermon.

Stay cool His way,
Lisa

Some weeks ago while standing in line for breakfast at an airport, I connected with a service worker behind a counter. She had been somberly going through her duties. Then briefly in a transaction with me, a flicker of life came to her face and eyes. It was as if she existed and mattered. Quickly she returned to a blank expression of dull routine. For a moment she had been visible. For a moment there had been humanity, followed soon by a retreat to the familiar, of being a low-wage, replaceable part in a system far bigger than both of us. That glimmer, along with last month's annual diocesan clergy Lent event centered on Sabbath economics, reminded me of how invisible much of our national and world economies typically are.

In 1922, one of the leading American advertising copywriters, Helen Woodward, gave other copywriters some advice. "If you are advertising any product," she said, "never see the factory in which it was made... Don't watch the people at work ... Because, you see, when you know the truth about anything, the real inner truth -- it is very hard to write the surface fluff which sells it."

What we do with money, how we spend it, where we give it and invest it, and what return we get...all these and more are critical avenues for us to honor basic promises made in church to "seek and serve Christ in all people, loving our neighbors as ourselves "and to "respect the dignity of every human being." There is no restriction on whose people and where this seeking, serving and respecting is to occur. I think we are to be mindful of the products we buy and the products we invest in. It is worth considering whether or not these products balance well with bedrock values we espouse in church.

An aspect of following Jesus is a responsibility to connect the dots of our national and global economy. Under, before, behind and after every financial transaction are dozens of human beings, whether we see them or not.

In Christ,
The Rev. Verdery Kerr

When Harry Patch died, I took notice, but my stepfather, who is English and obsessed with the history of the two World Wars, pointed out just how extraordinary he was. Harry Patch was Britain's last survivor of the battles on the Western Front in World War I. His war experiences did not harden his heart to others, but instead deepened his convictions of the common humanity that we all share and of the senseless slaughter of humanity that war extracts. Whenever asked about the war, he always responded, "Remember the Germans." At his funeral, which he had planned, his coffin was draped in the Union Jack and was carried into the gorgeous Wells Cathedral by soldiers from The Rifles, the Army unit Patch fought for in Flanders, but the soldiers wore no weapons, not even ceremonial ones. His honorary pallbearers included soldiers in full dress uniform, but without weapons, from Germany, Belgium, and France. And a German diplomat read from 2 Corinthians 5: "...if anyone is in Christ, there is a new creation ... All this is from God, who reconciled us to himself through Christ, and has given us the ministry of reconciliation."

Harry Patch knew the difference between détente and reconciliation. By definition, détente is a relaxation of tension, but reconciliation is a restoration of harmony. In Christ, we are not called to simply tolerate one another, but to be reconciled with one another. Harmony is a musical term that does not mean one note, but many notes that complement one another to make a beautiful sound. In every aspect of our lives, we are called by Christ, not to a position of détente, but to a ministry of reconciliation. If Harry Patch could do that after fighting and being wounded at Ypres, surely we can too.

The Rev. Marty Hedgpeth

One of the beautiful things about our nation is that to become critical of it is to exercise the freedom of speech promised by it. My oldest child recently took a course on media law as part of her journalism major. She expected the class to be dull, but a few weeks into it, she gushes, "The Constitution is amazing, Mom. I am in awe of it."

The Fourth of July is days away, and I hope you have some plans to enjoy the day. On Sunday, we will sing from the "national songs" section of the hymnal. The first service read from The Book of Common Prayer on American soil occurred on June 19, 1579, near San Francisco, when Sir Francis Drake's crew landed. Two-thirds of the signers of the Declaration of Independence were Anglicans, albeit some only nominally.

Sometimes being a Christian and being an American are confused as being one and the same. Quite possibly, the United States may be the nation where we are the most free to practice Christianity, yet it may also be the nation where there exist the most temptations to compromise and corrupt our faith. Greg Boyd, author of "The Myth of a Christian Nation," writes "While all the versions of the kingdom of the world acquire and exercise power over others, the kingdom of God, incarnated and modeled in the person of Jesus Christ, advances only by exercising power under others. It expands by manifesting the power of self-sacrificial, Calvary-like love."

There are prayers for our nation in The Book of Common Prayer (pages 821-23). There is also a litany of thanksgiving for national life (pages 838-39) that is part praise and part confession. The litany recognizes the gifts of our nation, its history and people, and also our propensity to distort and exploit those gifts. I encourage you to wave the red, white and blue this weekend as proud Americans; I certainly will be. I also encourage you to pray the BCP thanksgiving for national life as a Christian who knows that being Christlike, and being what is culturally defined as good and just and right in America, are often in conflict.

+Lisa

Three or four weeks ago some new information came in about the Middle School mission trip we had been planning for over a year. It seems our team of teens, to be led by Lauren Robbins, two fearless moms and a yet to be determined "male chaperone," were going to be doing some serious construction. The news had everyone a bit on edge. The packing list that arrived included various power tools that could maim or dismember, extension ladders, and the colorful request for "four cans of wasp spray for every five people!" The project our group would work on was also announced. It would build a roof over a porch, repair some shingles, paint, fix, mend and so forth. "Who is going to help us?" Lauren asked the program director. "The lady who owns the house will help," came the reply. "She's in her 80s!" replied Lauren, who had carefully read the ominous details of the trip.

I haven't gotten today's update, but I can tell you that the work is almost done and no teen has been wielding a reciprocating saw, much to their chagrin. How did it happen? Grace. Grace that the leadership came to include a new participant in our church family who had some construction experience and was willing to take last-minute vacation to join the work crew. God's grace was in the leadership of the trip that calmly drove the six hours to Franklin, West Virginia knowing that they would simply choose to do only the work that was suitable for their maturity and skill level and that their gifts would be enough. And there was the often understated grace of showing up.

Though the elderly lady's house has been in disrepair for some time, and though she was apparently loved by her neighbors and her community, nothing had been done. Nothing was done until our group showed up. Upon their arrival the whole community came forward with tractors, tools, and expertise. They came forward to do the work that our group could not and to teach our group how to do the work that they could. They came forward because of the grace that came from our group's willingness to go with God!

God didn't send Moses to Pharaoh because he was the most convincing speaker. God didn't wait for Jeremiah to grow up before he called him to be a prophet. The disciples didn't have any idea what they were getting into when Jesus asked them to follow him. But Moses, Jeremiah, the disciples, and our mission team all went where God called them. None of them knew exactly what they had to offer but trusted that God's "power working in us can do infinitely more than we can either ask or imagine." (Ephesians 3:20). May all of us be so brave as to go to a place, even in our own homes, and bring the grace of God that comes when you are willing to show up.

John Porter-Acee

Scene I: For years, two Christ Church parishioners sit a few pews apart from each other on Sunday mornings. They exchange the peace pleasantly with one another, but not their names or any other personal information. This is the 7:30 a.m. service, after all.

Scene II: One of those parishioners sits in a hospital waiting room. His daughter is having surgery that day. One of the physicians tending to his daughter passes by the waiting room. The father and the doctor look at each other, and then look again. They know each other. Where? Then recognition clicks. They have exchanged the peace with one another for years in the pews at Christ Church. This time when they shake hands, the peace is even more real, especially for the father. This doctor will take special care with his daughter.

In our daily life, I imagine there are people we each see regularly but know nothing about them: the person behind the counter at our favorite coffee shop, lunch spot, dry cleaners. The mail carrier who comes to our door each day. That person we see frequently in the elevator, parking lot, playground, walking the dog. How might it change things if we introduce ourselves, inquire about the other person's day, family? How might it affect the tone of our worship experience if we passed the peace as well as genuine interest in knowing one another?

There's a song that says "let peace begin with me." Today is the 63rd anniversary of the bombing of Hiroshima. It might be called dramatic to say that there is a connection between our willingness to extend a hand to someone we don't know and the tragedies of war, but I believe that peace is the deliberate adjustment of my life to the will and compassion of God. Where can you initiate a little peace this week?

Lisa +

I once saw on the notice board of St. James' Church, Piccadilly, London, this statement:

"A vision without a task is a dream.
A task without a vision is drudgery.
A vision and a task together is the hope of the world…"

"A vision and a task together is the hope of the world." I like the straight-forward pithiness of that. This wedding of task and vision is a good organizing principle for a life, a parish, a world.

As Jesus went about during the years of his public ministry, he never let his hearers doubt for a minute what his vision was, beginning with what Luke 4:16-30 records as his first sermon in his home-town synagogue. It was a very short sermon (those were the days). First he read from the scroll of the prophet Isaiah (61:1, 2, 58):

"The Spirit of the Lord is upon me,
because he has anointed me to bring good news to the poor.
He has sent me to proclaim release to the captives
and recovery of sight to the blind,
to let the oppressed go free,
to proclaim the year of the Lord's favor."

….so far so good….

Then Jesus added: "To day this scripture been fulfilled in your hearing," thus identifying himself as the one anointed and sent to do this ministry of proclamation, healing, and liberation. Those who heard him said something like, "Isn't this Joseph and Mary's boy all grown up? Who does he think he is?" For his presumptuousness, the people of Nazareth tried to throw him off a high cliff, a cautionary note for preachers ever since.

He was not to die that day, of course, but later, after his world had had three years to hear his vision and to witness his ministry of healing and teaching, tasks he set about to make incarnate his vision of a world made new, a world where justice and charity would embrace, where peace and freedom from fear and want would be enthroned, where word and deed would be perfectly aligned.

Melding a vision and task is a wonderful, life-giving organizing principle. By it, Jesus of Nazareth brought in the first fruits of God's reign, and the world could never be the same.

Jesus used this principle to teach by word and action that serving God opens to us a world of possibilities that otherwise simply does not exist. I doubt that he ever said anything like "organizing principle." It simply was the way he did his ministry.

I offer this to you as a way we can work to live our lives in this parish and in the world beyond, for only in this way will we be able to move forward in the direction that God is calling us to go, the direction of loving service freely and joyfully given.

The Rev. Nick White

It is said that Wednesday's child is full of woe. I think that it is during the middle of the night, and in the middle of the week, that our worries and fears weigh the heaviest. Perhaps it is an old wound that refuses to heal, or maybe since last Wednesday a new responsibility, disappointment or heartache has arisen. Sometimes by Wednesday we can even turn wonderful blessings into cause for concern and anxiety (what if I were to lose that blessing? could I be even happier?).

It is my experience that longing for a life where we have no worries is longing for a life without growth, without the joy of renewal, without knowing just how deep the light within us can shine.

If looking ahead, we notice looming mountains or turbulent waters, we can be overwhelmed by what we need to be able to cross them. Yet, we do not have to be fully equipped today for what we may need tomorrow or further down the road. There is a tradition on the Appalachian Trail called "trail magic." Seasoned and frequent hikers, as well as locals living near the Trail, will place candy or trail mix at spots along the trail for the next hiker along the way. Usually such discoveries seem to appear when they are needed the most -- unexpected care and energy for the next leg of the journey.

Maybe today you can think of a way to give someone else encouragement, support and hope. Maybe today you need to trust that whatever light and strength you will require for the days ahead will be given to you as you need them.

Lisa+

How many choices have you made today? Has it ever occurred to you that each choice you make, no matter how big or how small, marks a luxury in your life that many do not have? True poverty is a life without the ability or the power to choose.

In an effort to understand the impoverished of our city, many high school students will gather at Christ Church this Friday night to spend a night out in the cold. We will have a homeless man come and join us as a speaker and a construction consultant as we try to figure out how a cardboard box might provide shelter from the cold. I do not doubt for a second that Friday's lows in the upper 20s will open the eyes of our youth to the pain of the impoverished. I do, however, doubt that a true understanding of what it means to be poor could ever be achieved by those of us who are blessed with so many choices.

As we shiver in the cold we will be comforted by the thought that this is only for one night. We will be comforted by the knowledge that someone among us has the key to the Church and if it really got too bad they would certainly let us in. We will be comforted in no small way by the high dollar clothing and sleeping bags that we selected from our closets that overflow with resources. We are comforted and empowered by the many choices that we have in our day-to-day lives.

As we draw closer to Christ, may we come to see that those who have been left with few or no choice have a claim to make in our abundance. May we seek to serve Christ as we serve others and provide more opportunities for all people to have the luxury of choice in their lives. May we give people the opportunity to choose to work, to choose to get and stay healthy, to choose to live in a home that can be paid for by the wages they are able to earn. May we choose to use the power of our choices to empower those who have none, and all in the name of the One who chose to empty himself entirely so that we might be made whole.

The Rev. John Porter-Acee

Several baptisms stand out in my mind. The baptism I took part in last night is likely one I won't ever forget. The one baptized, Chris, is in his 60s. As I shared with those at the service last night, a baptism is not a naming ceremony, but a claiming ceremony. God claims us as his own, and gives us the option of claiming him right back. For several years now Chris has been sensing God's claim on him, God beckoning him to draw nearer, to trust him. Interesting to me is that Chris never realized until recent months that being a Christian also meant being a part of a community. More than just coming to worship on Sunday, he has chosen to come to Wednesday night classes, he's made friends, he's made a financial pledge, he's eager to begin confirmation classes in February. Chris has come to know that being a disciple is not a solitary activity. He was baptized last night into a community who promised to uphold him. It's what a spiritual home is supposed to feel like.

In a world where people are hungry, lonely, grieving, frightened, oppressed, a baptism makes the outrageous claim that not only does God love us, but that God's love has the power to heal, forgive, resurrect, make new, rebuild what's broken, give peace, foster hope, instill purpose and create communities of trust and joy. Thank you, Chris, for reminding me of God's claim on me and for inspiring me to claim him right back once again.

Lisa

Besides a perennial depiction of triumphant, tough men on screens who "chew nails" and "spit bullets," the only other prevailing portrait of men I see in media is a picture of ineptness, oafishness, irrelevance. It's as if there're only two models for manhood. One is prone to violence and divides the world into good guys/bad guys. The other is a buffoon. I confess to solace in the latter because clergy are usually shown to be similarly weak and ineffective.

Like many children of the 20th century, I grew up with an absent father. He, too, grew up with a father who was usually away. Business ownership, rising in the corporate world and a very strong work ethic dictated that 70 hours or more of work each week was necessary. It's what men were expected to do. Those long absences did not lessen one bit the hunger my siblings (a brother and two sisters) and I had for a strong, healthy, adult male in our lives. We sought this in all sorts of ways. Athletics was the primary venue I sought to fill the emptiness.

I'll not forget how stunned I was the first practice I held as the coach of a youth basketball team at the Sioux City, Iowa, YMCA. As a handful of children gathered around me, I realized what a massive responsibility this was. It wasn't about basketball or winning. To those children for a season I was God to them. How I treated them and what I asked of them mattered a lot.

This calling is not about being a soft, anything-goes Santa Claus. It's an honorable, holy calling to be present; to live and demand high standards, to give a steadiness and fairness and to lend a sound masculinity. Lots of times it has nothing to do with a level of education or amount of financial success. One in my history operated a gas station.

Christ Church has many such men. This is the one congregation I've served where numerous strong, healthy, fine men repeatedly and consistently step forward to guide and mentor those who are younger. Again and again I have seen evidence of their contributions with younger men, teens and children. I'm confident that much more of this occurs here than I'll ever know.

Despite foolish, fanciful examples of men that dominate the media, this world still hungers for strong, steady men of high standards.

"Train children in the right way, and when old, they will not stray." (Proverbs 22:6).

In Christ,
Verdery

Holidays and Holy Days

I saw a commercial the other day that made me smile. Members of a family are searching for something high and low throughout their cluttered house. The husband locates a piece of paper, holds it up in the air, and declares, "I found it!" The others rush to him. The piece of paper reads: "New Year's Resolutions: #1 Eat healthy. #2 Exercise more. #3 Get organized." The wife then says, "Maybe we ought to move #3 to the top of the list."

My husband would certainly vote for that! I'm not very fond of making New Year's resolutions because I feel like I am setting myself up for disappointment. I have much more success keeping a Lenten discipline for 40 days. Short-term goals require short-term discipline and short-term self-control. But I like how the start of a new year feels fresh, anything seems possible, and I wonder what completely unexpected and unimaginable surprises of goodness will be discovered this year. Of course, I also wonder what unforeseen pain I will encounter.

By next year this time, I will be changed by the events and experiences of the year, just as I am changed since last year. I am still growing, I trust. Frederick Buechner suggests that growing up means growing in holiness. That seems rather presumptuous, doesn't it? And yet, as followers of Jesus, where else would we be headed? Buechner says if God has his way with us, we are going to be holy. To me, growing in holiness not only means that I will be more patient and kind, but my trust in God's ways will grow.

My dependence upon God will deepen, as will the time I spend seeking his presence. I will more readily forgive myself and others. I will grow in confidence that I have something uniquely to offer that the world needs, and I will find pleasure in giving it.

I am glad for this community at Christ Church and that, together this year, we can grow up into holiness. Just knowing that we have each other for help and love along the way makes me feel I'm at least on holy ground.

May it be a holy new year for us all.

Lisa+

My father was a high school teacher, and one day when he was being observed professionally in class, he introduced his students to the guest observer by saying the gentleman was there to watch a "master teacher at work." He expected his students to chuckle at this, but instead they didn't crack a smile and sat still, looking up attentively. Then one petite blonde in the class raised her hand and asked sweetly, "Mr. Goodwin, does this mean we won't be playing bingo again today?"

We all like to look good in front of our superiors, and we also like to find shortcuts to looking good and being good. Jesus, of course, is the master teacher, and he gave out several demanding assignments, including the most difficult of all -- to love one another. And from the very beginning, Jesus' disciples have been trying to pin down exactly what the assignment means, in an effort to make the best grade possible and to be certain no more is done than is needed. One of Jesus' most interested pupils heard the assignment to love your neighbor and quickly asked for specifics. "Who is my neighbor?" he asked. The disciple Peter shot up his hand and got right to the rub of it, "How many times do I have to forgive someone?"

Valentine's Day focuses on romantic love, which is a complicated, wondrous and, yes, a many-splendored thing. Yet we can survive without **eros** or romantic love (interestingly, the word **eros** is not found in scripture), but the kind of love Jesus calls us to is vital to our health and wholeness. The commandment to love one another, **agape** love, is given as much for own sake as for those we might love. When Paul talks of love in the famous passage from 1 Corinthians so often read at weddings, it is not romantic love, but spiritual love, **agape** -- love that is sacrificial and forbearing, love that is an act of will, not of emotion.

The commandment to love one another is not a test but a gift. For, you see, the grades are already in, and we passed with flying colors. The commandments of God are not to prove our worthiness and value to God, but to **give** our life worth and value. We are free to love without regard to margins, to costs, or to whether our love will be accepted, appreciated or will ever accomplish anything the world values. Jesus taught that when you love your neighbor -- bingo! -- it is the same as loving yourself.

The Rev. Lisa Saunders

I read that President Harry Truman wrote a letter to his wife, Bess, every day they spent apart -- some 1,300 letters over the course of their marriage. Some might say, cynically, that their marriage flourished because they were apart 1,300 days and not because he wrote her 1,300 letters.

Valentine's Day, at its very worst, is a florist and greeting card industry scam; at its very best, today is a prompt to do something loving for another person. In the famous scripture passage about love found in 1 Corinthians 13, each of the sixteen descriptions of love is a verb in the original Greek.

Love is always something you do. "Love" the feeling is the fruit of "love" the verb. Jesus never talked about the romantic love that is the focus of commercialized Valentine's Day. Jesus talked about love that is marked by sacrifice and forbearance. Jesus talked about the love that he has for us and that he wants us to have for one another, not to make your life difficult, but so "your joy may be complete." (John 15:10-11)

Any day is a good day to speak to or write to someone who has encouraged you, mentored you, inspired you, been patient with you, made you laugh, helped you cry. But today might be an especially good day for it.

Love and peace,
Lisa

Today is Ash Wednesday. I imagine most of you know that the ashes we use today are made from burning the palms we waved on Palm Sunday. We waved those palms to acknowledge Jesus as King and Savior, to proclaim our allegiance to Jesus. But it isn't long before we lose our way and no longer love, serve or honor God's ways.

Ash Wednesday is the day we gather as one body and say with one voice, "We have lost our way." The church's technical word for this is "repentance." The ashes point to the sooty nature of our existence, our brokenness and charred efforts to love well. But the ashes also point to our creation; we are created from the dust of the earth. Ashes are all the material God needs to create life. We will bear on our foreheads both an acknowledgement of our own inability to get things right, and God's ability to set things right.

Lent becomes a season designed to help us find our way again. We take on disciplines that might draw us closer to God, that put us on a path more likely to lead us to God's truth for us. We put our treasures and pleasures down for a season, and reflect on who we are in the deepest places of our hearts and souls. I offer some questions to reflect upon for discerning your own Lenten discipline. (They come from the Rev. Tambria Lee, associate rector at Chapel of the Cross in Chapel Hill.)

Presence: What habit do I currently have that blocks my access to God?
Prayer: Do I make room in my day for some form of prayer?
Relationship: How am I at "being the Christ" in the world?
Body: How am I taking care of my body?
Resources: How do I use my resources of time, talent and treasure?

I invite you to the observance of a holy Lent.

Lisa+

Recently a colleague brought to my attention an ancient Cherokee tale. A Cherokee grandfather confided in his granddaughter that there was always a battle inside him. It was a fight between two wolves. One wolf incarnated ignoble characteristics such as envy, greed, arrogance, guilt, inferiority, anger, resentment, self-pity. The other wolf brought forth joy, humility, peace, love, hope, courage, generosity, faith, compassion. The granddaughter asked, "Which wolf is winning?" The elder Cherokee replied, "The one I feed."

The season of Lent begins today with Ash Wednesday. The text for this service (especially the Litany of Penitence) in the Prayer Book (pp. 264-269) is my favorite of all the various liturgies in the Church. I find the words not a "downer" at all. Rather they are an instrument for health, for coming clean, for standing tall henceforth and anew with God and Jesus to be about bold, audacious things in this world. Ash Wednesday and Lent are summons to new beginnings, to reminders to be fully awake and aware of ourselves, others, the Lord. It's a wake-up call not to succumb to "automatic pilot" in our living, to ramp up our intentionality to live in this world with our many things, pressures, expectations (those we impose on ourselves and those presented to us from outside) more so with the priorities of Jesus at the center.

I encourage us to be conscious about which "wolf" we are feeding. I encourage us to draw from those old, traditional Lenten disciplines of (1) regular prayer, study and devotions; (2) fasting from spiritual and material appetites and from attitudes unworthy of Christ; (3) generosity with ourselves and with our resources. That we go about these disciplines both solely and in community is essential.

In Christ,
Verdery

Behold, O Lord God, our strivings after a truer and more abiding order. Give us visions that bring back a lost glory to the earth, and dreams that foreshadow the better order which you have prepared for us. Scatter every excuse of frailty and unworthiness; consecrate us all with a heavenly mission; open to us a clear prospect of our work. Give us strength according to our day gladly to welcome and gratefully to fulfill it. Amen.

In the Creole language of Haiti, the verb *karem* names the action of removing a boat from the water -- dry-docking it -- to scrape, recaulk, clean, and repair it to make the boat once again sea-worthy and reliable. The exact same word -- *karem* -- names this season of Lent, this time of putting ourselves into drydock for the kind of examination and overhauling God calls us to undergo and which we know we need. The metaphor is a compelling one for it conveys a sense of stripping ourselves down so that God can remake us, recaulk us, from stem to stern.

This season of Lent is about reorienting ourselves, about waiting upon the Lord to see what plans he might have in mind for us rather than insisting that only our plans and computations matter.

Early in the 1800s, Eleazer Hull was New Bedford's most successful and daring whaling captain. He had no formal training or schooling, but he consistently sailed the farthest, brought home the largest catch, and suffered the least casualties to crew and ship. When asked how he navigated so successfully, Captain Hull responded, "I go up on deck, get the drift of the sea, listen to the wind in the rigging, take a long look at the stars, and then set my course."

One day, the insurance underwriters insisted that all captains they would cover had to have formal training in navigation. Captain Hull had to go to school or be dismissed. So off he went to get his formal training, and thence back to sea. On returning from his first voyage as an educated, certified navigator, again with the greatest catch, someone asked him how he liked his new formal system of sailing. "It's wonderful," he said. "I go to my cabin and get out the charts, work through the proper calculations, and then set a course with mathematical precision. Then I go up on deck, get the drift of the sea, listen to the wind in the rigging, and take a long look at the stars. And then I go below and correct my computations."

Lent is our time for going below to correct our computations, for getting the drift of our living, listening to the wind in the rigging and taking a long look at the heavens and at ourselves. How are things going for you in your spiritual drydock? If you're like most of us, you resist the kind of searching self-examination to which we are called.

Some of us still live by the credo of another time: "Every day in every way I'm getting better and better." That doesn't work when the diagnosis comes back cancer -- or the promotion falls through -- or a child or a spouse or a friend wanders off into some cockeyed nirvana -- or you discover that downsizing means you don't have a job any more -- or the meaning and joy of a relationship have drifted away and you didn't even notice it until one day they just weren't there.

Some of us live in a state of denial about whatever it is that stands between us and the fulfillment for which we yearn, the meaning we seek. But in the darkness of the night comes the realization that all for which we have so mightily struggled means nothing without spiritual and emotional richness.

Some of us figure we have everything we need, and we've earned it the old-fashioned way -- we've worked for it. Those are the ones who have trouble seeing that their keels need checking and repainting and who haven't checked the wind and the stars lately.

Each of us has at least a bit of all of the above. Maybe this could be the Lent when we strip away some defenses and turn off some taped scripts, to be still, to seek centeredness, where we might see the stars and hear the wind in the rigging and correct our carefully wrought but misleading calculations.

The Rev. Nicholson B. White

In the Catechism found in the back of our Book of Common Prayer we learn that a sacrament is an outward and visible sign of an inward and spiritual grace. Sacraments are at their very best when you can find their point of juxtaposition with the world around you. I experienced my most sacramental moment as a "baby priest" one week ago today.

I was invited to celebrate at the Ash Wednesday service for Trinity Episcopal School. A parade of nearly 400 K-8th graders approached the altar rail to receive the imposition of ashes. Outside of this liturgy it would be quite painful, sickening, in fact, to look into the vibrant faces of child after child and think of their deaths. Jesus, however, allows us to turn the world upside down. I did not have in my mind's eye the Hollywood image of a weeping family dressed in black, huddled around a grave, as a stranger casts dirt onto a casket. My ears did not hear the refrain of "Earth to earth, ashes to ashes, dust to dust" mixed in with sobs.

My ears heard the words of St. Paul in 1 Corinthians 15, mixed in with John Donne's poem "Death Be Not Proud."

"Death be not proud, though some have called thee
mighty and dreadfull, for, thou art not so,
for, those, whom thou think'st, thou dost overthrow,
die not, poore death, nor yet canst thou kill me.
From rest and sleepe, which but thy pictures bee,
much pleasure, then from thee, much more must flow,
and soonest our best men with thee doe goe,
rest of their bones, and soules deliverie.
Thou art slave to Fate, Chance, kings, and desperate men,
and dost with poyson, warre, and sicknesse dwell,
and poppie, or charmes can make us sleepe as well,
and better then thy stroake; why swell'st thou then;
one short sleepe past, wee wake eternally,
and death shall be no more; death, thou shalt die."

1 Cor. 15:55: "Where, O death, is your victory? Where, O death, is your sting?"

I did not weep for the faces of the children as I assured every last one of them that they would indeed die one day. My heart, instead, hoped with joy that they might hear in my words the freedom Christ has offered us from our mortal bodies. Imagine the future of our world if but one of them heard and believed that they are not slaves to their flesh, for it will surely pass away.

The Rev. John Porter-Acee

I received a phone call this week from a parishioner in my last parish. He had been at the funeral of Rico Arcari, who had served that parish as sexton for many years, including my time there. In his obituary, Rico had requested that "in lieu of flowers, please take the time to contact a friend or loved one and express your gratitude for his or her place in your life." So this friend from so long ago called me. It was a simple gesture that was full of grace, and it made my day.

Lent begins today. If you are wondering what to do to mark the season, I highly recommend what my former sexton suggested. Contact by phone or letter or email or even in person those who have blessed your life in some way. Perhaps the greatest lesson of penitence is not realizing how much we sin or mess up, but realizing how much we are loved and forgiven by God and by countless family and friends.

In this holy season of self-examination and penitence, try giving thanks to those who have loved and forgiven you. I promise it will make for a humbling and joyful season.

The Rev. Marty Hedgpeth

The Gospel reading for this first Sunday in Lent is the story of Jesus being tempted by the devil at the end of his 40 days in the desert (Luke 4:1-13). The story is bookended by a description of the times that the devil comes to call on us. The story begins as the devil appears to Jesus when Jesus has gone without food for 40 days and is famished. The story ends by the devil deciding to leave until another "opportune time." I might be particularly sensitive to this message as I am in the process of leaving for a sabbatical, but I truly believe this story is important for us in all seasons of our life and especially in this season of Lent.

When we are malnourished we should expect the devil to come calling. Jesus, who as a reminder is the Son of God, was able to fend the devil off even when he was empty and without nourishment, but there is no reason for us to expect that we can do the same thing. Jesus knew that he needed more than material food as nourishment. Jesus knew that fame and power and wealth were not going to feed his soul either. What may have been the most amazing thing that Jesus did not fall for though was the devil's temptation to test God in the midst of Jesus' famine. Even when Jesus was hungry, tired, and in danger, Jesus knew that God was still with him. Jesus knew that God would still save him, bless him, and feed him. Jesus was smart enough not to test God with the ever so familiar "if God really loves me then He will certainly do this," temptation.

How will each of you take this season of Lent to seek true nourishment for your life and your soul? How will you try to rely less on the "junk food" the world offers us in fame, fortune and power? How will you grow to trust in God's never failing goodness and His ability to save even as you teeter on the tip of disaster? I can actually assure you that I will be about seeking nourishment this Lent and for the remainder of the sabbatical that the people of Christ Church are blessing me with. May each of you be so blessed to find this season as one that you can feed your soul, as well.

John M. Porter-Acee III

For the second time in my adult life, I have begun to take piano lessons, which I never took as a child. I have now reached the point where both hands have to play at the same time and both hands have to find notes that are farther and farther apart. At my last lesson, my teacher noted that I was taking my fingers off the keys too far and as a result, I got lost. He had me keep my fingers lightly on the keys, like home base, which enabled me to know where they were, thus I was able to figure out what keys to go to next far more easily. It really worked!

I think one of the important exercises of Lent is training ourselves to stay close to Jesus, our ultimate home base, which helps us better orient ourselves as to where we are meant to go next and what we are meant to do next. Far too often the world seduces us into straying far from home and finding ourselves lost, we don't even know which way to turn. The Gospel, the good news is that when that happens, our good Lord comes searching for us.

We can rejoice that God never abandons us, but we can also grow as disciples of Christ and do less wandering off. My piano teacher wrote on each page of my next lesson, "Hang on to the piano." This Lent, I suggest we all try to hang on to Jesus a little bit more day by day. As Dorothy said, "There's no place like home."

Marty

Though the world is on all our minds and we all seek companions or guides in our current journey, it is difficult to walk as a community in a way that meets everyone right where they are. With the economy, some are struggling but have time to recover before retirement, some have left retirement to go back to work, some have had to totally change their hopes and goals for now and the future, and some have been going through these struggles for the past decade without the communal concern and support that is being given today. Everyone seems to be in a different place. God calls us into community to bear each other's burdens. God wants us to walk hand-in-hand to serve one another and the world but we must first find where our paths intersect so that we may gather together as one. It is time for us to meet at the foot of the Cross.

Each Lent we are invited to meet each other at the foot of the Cross. Each Lent we are invited to return to the place where all of our paths begin, intersect, end and begin again. Millions will kneel throughout the world today and have the sign of the Cross drawn upon their heads. Millions will hear the words today that invite us to remember that we all began when God breathed His life into the dust of the Earth. We remember as a community of believers today that a time will come when our life will leave the matter of our mortal home but through the Cross our life does not come to an end.

The ashes of Ash Wednesday remind us of the temporal nature of our lives here on Earth but the cross that they depict on our foreheads reminds us of the love of Christ that conquers all. No matter where we are on our personal journeys, if we return to the Cross this Lent we will have a common beginning. No matter what obstacles we face as individual families, our collective family has already overcome every obstacle through Christ and will forever hold in common the love of God found in Christ Jesus. As Paul wrote to the Romans:

"Who will separate us from the love of Christ? Will hardship, or distress, or persecution, or famine, or nakedness, or peril, or sword? No, in all these things we are more than conquerors through him who loved us. For I am convinced that neither death, nor life, nor angels, nor rulers, nor things present, nor things to come, nor powers, nor height, nor depth, nor anything else in all creation, will be able to separate us from the love of God in Christ Jesus our Lord." (Romans 8:35, 37-39)

The Rev. John M. Porter-Acee III

In my rooting around for something good to read this Lent, I spent some time turning the pages of "In the Company of Christ" by Benedicta Ward. At one point Ward writes "To be there at all on the way to the Cross, the heart must be broken open, not broken down." In my 10 minutes worth of rambling sermon this past Sunday, I may have only been trying to say just that.

As we walk whatever path we are on, even the path to the Cross during Holy Week, God desires so much more from us than the recognition of our unworthiness. Don't be fooled: our understanding of self as sinner and sinful is a prerequisite for what God dreams for us, but it is not the end in and of itself. God does not leave us at the place in our journey where we find our own sin; it is from this place that God offers us the most beautiful and revealing view of the Cross. It is from the place that we recognize our sin that we learn the most beautiful and revealing aspects of God's love for us.

Come to the cross. Come through grace with the bravery to hold your head high enough to gaze upon the mystery. Do not come beaten down and full of self-hate. Pray for the grace to come not only fully aware of who you are, but also fully present, hiding nothing from God or yourself. May your heart then be broken open with the overflowing and uncontainable realization that it is you, exactly as you are, not only for whom Christ died, but for whom Christ has unfailing and unwavering love.

The Rev. John M. Porter-Acee III

When we baptize people in the Episcopal Church we take some oil that has been blessed by a Bishop (chrism) and we make the sign of the cross on the forehead of the person getting baptized while saying: "You are sealed by the Holy Spirit in baptism and marked as Christ's own forever." Last Wednesday, many people came to church to receive a very different sign of the cross on their forehead. On Ash Wednesday, the sign of the cross is made with the ashes of burnt palm branches from the previous year's celebration of Palm Sunday. They are applied while saying: "Remember that you are dust, and to dust you shall return." The truth is that the two crosses have a lot more in common than one might quickly assume.

It may not seem necessary, at first, to try to make the cross of baptism relate to the cross of Ash Wednesday but I would go so far as to say that it is only through understanding the immersion of our baptism that we can begin to understand the ashes of Lent. Our life in Christ exists in parallel to the past, present, and future deaths of our bodies. When we are baptized, we are baptized into the life and death of Christ. We intricately link ourselves to Christ's life everlasting, and Christ's death to the world and sin. It is our promise of life in Christ that allows us to see beyond our bodies and our "worldly desires." It is the gift of love we receive in baptism that begins to teach us to seek eternal things, like friendship, trust, and joy, as opposed to shackling our bodies to the pursuit of temporal pleasures.

In Lent, as we journey closer to the Cross of Christ, we are offered an opportunity to examine ourselves in terms of the crosses that we bear. Have we accepted God as our Father, and not forgotten that we have been marked as His own forever? Have we allowed our bodies to take second chair to our spirits, realizing that our bodies are but dust? Our lives are not without purpose. There is much treasure to be sought after and won. Our crosses remind us that we have eternity to look forward to, and that some treasures will last longer than others. Christ's Cross shows us the supreme treasures of love and forgiveness as he beckons us to follow Him.

The Rev. John M. Porter-Acee III +

Lent is a season of self examination and spiritual growth. But how do we grow? I have learned there are four ingredients that are essential if any real growth is to happen in our lives. These ingredients are truth, grace, accountability and time.

Truth. What is the truth of our lives? Unfortunately, we run from the truth. We deny it. We can't seem to face it. But the truth is the truth. And the "truth shall set us free." We can't treat the illness until we know what it is. But once we do, we begin the process of healing and transformation.

Grace. Grace is God's statement to us that He is big enough to deal with all of our worst problems. God is big, and nothing surprises Him. He is the God "from whom no secrets are hid." He has seen it all. His grace comes from both His commitment to us as well as His promise to support and strengthen us through every experience and test in life. His grace abounds and is "sufficient for thee."

Accountability. Everybody needs to be held accountable. How are we held accountable? The reading of scripture holds us accountable. The truth in scripture helps show us the light of where we are and what we can become. Friends and family also hold us accountable. There is no such thing as "self help." We need each other. Accountability is more than someone getting in our face. It is the love and encouragement of Christian brothers and sisters who are there for us, and promise to walk beside us through the storms and the nights.

Time. "Rome was not built in a single day." Once we figure out the truth, accept God's grace, surround ourselves with friends, we need to remember the importance of time. Growth takes seasons. Often it is one step back. Two steps forward. Three steps back. Two steps forward. But we do grow. So be patient. It will happen in time. Trust God.

A blessed Lent to you.

Love and Prayers,
Chip

Just as I sat down to write an e-devotion, I got a call from a friend in my last parish telling me of the untimely death of a member of that parish, a man who was only a few years older than I. He was a man of deep faith, a man who served with me in parish leadership, a man who was a dear friend. It is hard to think of living in a world where Bob Joyce is absent and I regret not having a recent and last conversation with him, but at least I know that through the communion of saints in heaven and on earth, we will always be together.

Bob's death reminded me of what one of our parishioners does for the forty days of Lent -- he sends notes to people whose lives have influenced his own -- one person, one note for each day of Lent. I love this idea and have tried to do it myself, but I invariably mess up. I'm going to try it again because there are so many people, like Bob, who have nurtured my faith by their lives. Rowan Williams has written, "Faith has a lot to do with the simple fact that there are trustworthy lives to be seen, that we can see in some believing people a world we'd like to live in."

Perhaps the greatest discipline we can cultivate in Lent and throughout life is that of outward, thankful acknowledgment of those who have revealed that divine world and shared our journey. Take the time to thank them and be amazed at how rich you are.

Marty

I was about to get on an airplane for a return home flight, and I had read all the books I brought with me. I raced into an airport bookstore for a quick purchase. The book, "Sight Hound" by Nancy Houston, proved to be a gift.

In the book, a grandmother asks her granddaughter, "What do you think makes people happy?" After the granddaughter makes a guess or two, the grandmother responds, "Not fame, not money, not work, not art…not even love… All of these things can be nice, even money. They will make you happy for ten minutes each, but ten minutes isn't long, held next to a life." Pressed, the grandmother finally gives her the answer. "Generosity." Being generous makes people happy. As the grandmother explains, "Happiness that lingers is not the face the world turns to you… It is the face you turn to the world."

These Lenten days are usually observed with a certain denial and sacrifice, not to help us learn how to live more sparingly, but to help us learn how to live more fully. We recognize that what gives life its value, worth and sweetness has more to do with what we bring to the table than what we take away. Jesus' ministry was a complete self-giving. Generosity colored everything he did and said. The face he turned to the world was filled with unwavering and undiminishing love.

Another novelist, Reynolds Price, was asked if he harbored any regrets. His reply: "I regret only my economies." And isn't it true, that when we opt to be tight-fisted -- not just with our money, but with our time and attention, our kindness and understanding, our love and service -- we only find ourselves regretting our smallness and our ultimately useless economies? Generosity led Jesus to Calvary, a way he promises also leads to life in all its abundance.

My hastily selected novel had immediate relevancy for me. Seated beside me on the plane was a mother with her over-tired, squirming 15-month-old son. I had nothing to offer her but a generous spirit. It helped all three of us.

The Rev. Lisa Saunders

This past weekend I was a co-leader of a retreat exploring poetry about death and resurrection. I am an old hand at retreats, having made them regularly throughout my ministry and before. I love to go settle in at a monastery and be silent for days on end, poring over scripture, praying and worshiping with the monks. But on this retreat we were looking at poetry -- a literary form that I avoided like the plague as an English major. And in the periods of silence, we were encouraged to do what we wanted from being silent to doing something creative -- work with clay, paint, etc. It was a time that challenged me to get way, way out of my comfort zone. I discovered that poetry can often express faith issues better than theology. In the periods of silence, I decided to continue the adventure, and I made a collage. I started out fairly disconnected with the activity, but I became more and more intrigued. I found myself unable to break away from it. And I love the result so much, I'm going to laminate my masterpiece!

There is a point in confessing all of this. We are entering into the final days of Lent and moving steadily toward the most holy days of our Christian year. Rather than simply observe these days the same old ways, I encourage you to step out of your comfort zone and try something new: Go to a worship service you have never experienced, such as Tenebrae or the Easter Vigil; forgive someone you vowed you would never forgive; do volunteer work at a shelter or a soup kitchen that is located somewhere you have never been before. To step out of our familiar worlds is to do precisely what Jesus did in journeying to his death in Jerusalem -- it is to live by faith, trusting less in ourselves and more in God. To venture into the unknown is to be open to the possibility of being changed, being transformed, and that is precisely what Christians are called to do.

The Rev. Marty Hedgpeth

It is a long way from Passion Sunday to Easter. It's the longest way in the world.

It's a way that begins with jubilant shouts of "Hosanna!" and ends with the words which forever signaled the utter end of things as the world had known them -- "He is not here. He is risen."

In between comes a blur of images, a din of voices, of hopes, fears, betrayals, and love.

"You have made my Father's house a den of thieves." "Thirty pieces of silver...." "My heart is ready to break with grief." "Let this cup pass from me." "Could none of you stay awake with me one hour?" "The Son of Man is betrayed to sinners." "The one I kiss is your man; seize him." "I do not know the man. I do not know the man. I do not know the man." "Are you the King of the Jews?" "*Eli, eli, lema sabachtani.*" "Father, into thy hands I commend my spirit."

From the ironic triumph of Palm Sunday...to the humiliation, pain, abject aloneness, betrayal, shame, and death of Holy Week -- to the empty tomb of Easter is a long, long way, as long as life itself -- as painful as life itself -- as confusing, as triumphant, as hopeful as life itself.

For the way Jesus walked, and the way he leads us, is the way to life, the only way to life.

And the way leads through Holy Week, which is not just a piece of the calendar or a ritually observed preamble to Easter, an awkward pause between high moments, but a holy time God gives us so that we may learn the lessons of meekness, of surrender, by seeing Jesus' own way of strong, trusting, triumphant meekness as the way to life grasped and lived joyfully, abundantly.

This is a different sort of meekness -- obviously -- born of strength, springing from infinite trust that God can indeed be trusted to do what God has promised, to love us to the end and then far beyond the end, beyond time, holding us in a way beyond mystery in the tenderness of his love.

If you want to know something of this love, walk the holy way of Holy Week so that you come to Easter's dawning of the gladsome promise of love ready to receive it and willing to empty self of self, as Jesus did, so that God can fill you brimful and overflowing.

God bless you and those you love in this holy season.

The Rev. Nick White

A parishioner, who prefers to remain anonymous, called me the week before Easter. "Is there anyone at Christ Church who is going to be alone at Easter that our family could invite to join us for lunch on Sunday?" she asked.

"Carol" went on to say that her family of four, plus her mother who was visiting, would be there, but that her table could seat far more. Perhaps someone at church would like to join them.

I gave her the name of two women I thought might welcome her invitation. One has no family, had been ill for some time but was much improved. The other woman is widowed, has no children in town, is homebound and has Parkinson's disease.

Carol, with the large table and big heart, called both women, and each accepted the invitation with enthusiasm. Carol had never met either woman, and of course, vice versa. One guest drove herself to the lunch and brought with her a delicious English trifle she made to share. The other guest was picked up by Carol's husband and brought to their home. Carol and her husband also invited another couple to lunch along with a single colleague of her husband's. The table was full for Easter lunch. As you might hope and expect, it was a wonderful occasion.

"I hope you can come back next Easter," said Carol's 10-year-old son as the women left. One of them told me that not only did she thoroughly enjoy the gathering, but that Easter lunch was the first home-cooked meal she had eaten in two years.

At Easter, we celebrate that God brings everyone to his table of mercy and abundance. Table fellowship was a frequent theme in Jesus' ministry on earth. Carol claims she didn't do anything special. It's true that preparing a meal is often mundane work, but who we invite to the table in our dining room is very close to who we invite to the table of our heart. Maybe next Easter, no one in our parish will spend the day alone.

Lisa+

How do we believe in goodness in the face of so much that is bad in our world?

Archbishop Desmond Tutu and his youngest daughter have written a wonderful book called "Made For Goodness" that explores this question. No stranger to the horrors of life, Archbishop Tutu spent many years on the Truth and Reconciliation Commission, a government sponsored group charged with listening to the testimony of those ravaged by apartheid. Though frequently devastated by the stories of evil, Tutu never lost hope.

What keeps Archbishop Tutu upbeat and optimistic? Over the years I have had two occasions to hear him speak. Each time he was asked this question. And each time he answers he answered the question the same way: "I believe people are fundamentally good and I believe that God is good. I place my ultimate trust in God. And because I believe, I can be happy, even excited about the future."

During this season of Easter, we realize that we are not alone in facing the challenges of life. Christ has risen to help us face them. Though it can be confusing at times, in the wake of bad news, God is always present, doing great and good things through people who say "yes" to God. Archbishop Tutu is one of those people. You are one of those people too! Through your works of love and determination, you become agents of the resurrection.

We were made for goodness -- to do good and creative things with God. In the end, God's acts at Easter teach us that death is not the most powerful force in life. Love is. When we believe this truth, we can love through life with confidence and hope.

With love and prayers,
Chip

At Easter, we find that God has figured out a way to say that all is well between us. We could not make things right with God, so God does it for us. This is the heart of our faith: there is nothing outside of God's power to transform, redeem, give life made new. This is revealed to us through the passion and resurrection of Jesus Christ. The miracle of Easter is not the removal of our pain and suffering -- to do so would mean the amputation of our free will, core to our humanity. The miracle Easter provides is finding life again on the other side of our pain, on the other side of the cross.

A man who had spoken out and worked for civil rights in apartheid South Africa and lived in exile for twenty years lost his arm and his eye in a car bomb. He was asked, "Didn't you ever have feelings of wanting revenge?" He said: "Not at all. I felt a sense of freedom, waking up from the accident and knowing I still had 95% of my body. You just keep your eyes on the prize, which is forgiveness and transformation. I feel like there are roses and lilies growing from this stump where my arm used to be."

Yes, that is the beautiful paradox and miracle of Easter. As we say in our Eucharistic prayer: In Jesus, God has delivered us out of error into truth, out of sin into righteousness, out of death into life. There is no point at which new life -- satisfying, meaningful life -- is not possible, and there is no point at which God will declare us beyond or beneath his saving grace. Alleluia indeed.

The Rev. Lisa Saunders

Last Sunday at the Discovery Service I taught the children why eggs are an Easter symbol. I explained that Jesus was dead in the big tomb and then on Easter he came out alive. Then I told a story of a caveman who discovered what seemed like a very light rock that he took home and put on top of a pile of rocks. I dramatically described how one day the "rock" began to move, then crack, then roll off the other rocks, and then split open. The children were amazingly attentive and I said, "And guess what appeared out of that cracked rock?" Out of the silence, a little girl in the back whispered, "Jesus!" Of course the answer I expected was a baby chicken, but the answer I got was far better.

The miracle of Easter is that the risen Christ does appear at times and in places when we are expecting something or someone else or are expecting nothing. When Mary went to the tomb to anoint Jesus, she was expecting a corpse. When Cleopas and his companion walked home to Emmaus and encountered a stranger whom they invited in for dinner, they expected no more than an acquaintance to break bread with them. When the disciples went fishing, they weren't expecting any help from the beach. All of them were surprised by the risen Lord.

Remember: Like those first disciples, the place to encounter the risen Lord is in our very ordinary, everyday lives. Like that little girl in church on Sunday, be open to the miracle that the risen Lord will appear. He will. Christ is risen. The Lord is risen indeed. Alleluia.

The Rev. Martha Hedgpeth

Since it is the Easter season until the Day of Pentecost, I want to tell you an Easter story.

Diana and I spent several months in spring 1992 in Port Elizabeth, South Africa, where I served as an itinerant supply priest, in and out of many congregations and languages. On Easter morning, I took the early service at St. Hugh's Church, a suburban white church. Then we raced off to the so-called black township of New Brighton, to assist a friend, Elliot Banzana, at his parish's 9:00 a.m. service, always a huge affair, but even bigger and grander on Easter.

In 1992, Nelson Mandela was out of prison, but the promised free elections were still two years away. In many ways, South Africa still struggled under the incomprehensible burden of apartheid, that evil of constitutionally mandated and protected, systemic racial inequality. The township system kept the traces apart (it still does, to a great extent), meaning, among other things, that opportunities for education, employment, and free movement were dreams for those not born to white privilege.

The service was in Xhosa, a musical language of clicks and inflections for which my mouth was clearly not made. My host said that I must preach and someone would translate. Clearly the translation was better than the preaching, judging from the congregation's enthusiastic responses to the very long renditions of my words. I told John's beloved story of Mary Magdalene coming to the garden's tomb on the third day, only to find her friend's body gone. She assumed that someone had spirited away Jesus' body before she could prepare it for a proper burial. As she walked, disconsolate, in the garden, she spotted a man whom she took to be the gardener. She didn't recognize him until Jesus said her name. In hearing her name, Mary was transformed -- and we and all creation with her.

Some of the good news for this black congregation, carried there by this white, middle-aged fellow from Ohio, as of course not really news, but the renewed proclamation of the Easter faith that God will bring life out of death, that Easter will always follow Good Friday, that Easter's light is conveyed to us one at a time as the risen Christ knows us and calls us each by name.

The Resurrection, that greatest mystery and of us can contemplate -- Easter's thundering truth that the power of God's love transforms all of life and all of death -- can touch us into life, as it touched Mary into life. The life is the light of God's love, and in that light there need be -- there will be -- no broken promises or relationships, no injustice, no *apartheid*, no deaths of love, trust, dreams, possibilities, for this Easter light has the power to weld together all that we and our systems have undone.

The dear people of New Brighton's Church of the Holy Spirit didn't need a seasonal celebration of newness. What they needed to hear once again was the promise of Easter: "Christ is risen and we are risen with him. The tomb's emptiness promises fullness of life that nothing -- no system, no government, no evil, not even our careless inattentiveness -- can take away from us." And the people of the Church of the Holy Spirit danced in the aisles because the news was so very good.

Christ is risen! He is risen indeed. And like Mary, like the people of New Brighton, we are risen with him. Alleluia Alleluia. Alleluia.

The Rev. Nick White

This is my favorite time of year. Spring is beginning to take hold, the days are getting longer, the birds are in overdrive, and spring training is full of hope and expectation. But even when all around us seems to be starting over, far too many of us are weighed down by thoughts of our own inadequacy and sinfulness. Most of us take our sins and brokenness very seriously, which is a good thing only if we ultimately move beyond them through repentance and to acceptance of the great gift of God's unconditional love and forgiveness.

The problem is that we often find it hard to believe that once forgiven, it really is forgotten and over. After all, I am not in the habit of forgiving and forgetting. I always remember long after the forgiveness. The great good news for us is that God, unlike us, really and truly does forgive and forget. There is a wonderful old story of a young girl in France several centuries ago who became very famous because God talked to her. So great did her fame become that the bishop was disturbed and he called the girl to his palace to question her. He could not get her to waver in her story, so he decided to find out the truth another way. He said, "The next time God talks to you, ask him what sin I described in my last confession." About a week later the girl was brought back before the bishop who asked her if she had talked with God. "Yes," she replied. "And what did he say when you asked about my confession?" the bishop asked. The young girl said, "I forgot." The bishop went into a rage, saying the girl was irresponsible. Finally the young girl managed to get the bishop's attention and she quietly said, "Sir, I did ask him and it was God who said, 'I forgot.'" At those words the bishop was speechless and ever thereafter he treated the girl as one of God's great saints. He knew she was right; he knew God had forgotten.

For each of us the promise is the same. When we turn to our good God and open before him all of our lives, warts and all, we are forgiven and then all is forgotten and our lives are just like the world around us on these early spring days -- full of new hope and bright new possibilities. Thanks be to God!

The Rev. Martha Hedgpeth

I had been down that street hundreds of times, but this time when I turned the corner on my bike, the street had been transformed. Tree branches (I don't know which kind of tree) heavy with peppermint pink blossoms curved over the road like the vaulting in a cathedral. The street was a carpet of pink petals that looked freshly strewn. The sun broke through the trees' limbs at an angle that cast a luminous glow; a slight breeze rustled the trees, and petals floated through the air like I was riding through a ticker tape parade. I thought to myself that I can travel far and wide across this globe but would be hard pressed to see something as beautiful as this spring sanctuary just two blocks from my house. About an hour later, I took my daughter to see this street, but the sun's light had shifted; there was no radiant glow. The petals on the road had been flattened by cars going by. The wind was still. The street looked completely unremarkable.

I am reading Barbara Brown Taylor's new book, "An Altar in the World," in which she writes about how the "earth is so thick with divine possibility that it is a wonder we can walk anywhere without cracking our shins on altars" -- places that mark the presence of God. Taylor calls to mind the story of Moses who did not run into a burning bush, but saw it from a distance and said, "I must turn aside and look at this great sight." Moses' choice to turn aside, to "park the sheep" he was tending and take a closer look at the bush changed his life and the course of history. If he had decided to return the next day to see if the bush was still burning, he might never have discovered what God had in mind for him.

Summertime is a wonderful time to turn aside from the distractions and discord in our lives, and to pay attention to God's flame flickering in the corner of our eye and the corner of our soul. We just may find ourselves standing before unlikely altars and coaxed into unlikely works of love and service.

Lisa

While Memorial Day is a holiday that observes the great sacrifice of men and women who served in the military to keep our nation one and free, it tends to be observed as the official beginning of summer. In our parish life members begin to attend church more sporadically and to travel off to vacation spots and to camp. As a result, parish life slows down a good bit: fewer Sunday services, no Church School, weekday classes end until fall, and the office even closes early on Fridays. Some consider this pure laziness and talk about how God doesn't go on vacation so the church should stay up and running full speed. I couldn't disagree more.

Sabbath time, the seventh day, was instituted as a part of creation. On that day God rested and called his creation, including us, to rest as well. In the course of a year, our lives are overstuffed with opportunities, challenges and responsibilities from September through May. (We are a school calendar, children-driven culture). But June through August is our Sabbath time. Nothing could be more important in our over-scheduled, goal-oriented, success-oriented community than for the church to say, "Stop. Slow down. Relax. Take the time to be recreated and renewed." And so two days into the "summer," I suggest we all do just that.

We will be here at church. There will be many opportunities to worship, study, serve, and be together. But whether you are here or not, take the time to observe the Sabbath of summer. "The earth is charged with the grandeur of God," says Gerard Manley Hopkins. Spend time discovering just that. Read a mystery. Take a walk after dinner. Sit and do nothing. It will be good for your spirit.

The Rev. Marty Hedgpeth

Summer is a great time for taking stock of our life with God. Do we feel we are growing towards God or away from God? Are we feeling hopeful? Do we trust God? Summer, with its longer days, gives us the chance to ask some important questions: is there an opportunity to rethink the way we have ordered our lives? Can we engage in spiritual practices that will lead us toward renewal and spiritual transformation?

In his book "A Testament of Devotion," Thomas Kelly writes: "Over the margins of life comes a whisper, a faint call, a premonition of richer living, which we know we are passing by. Strained by the very made pace of our daily outer burdens, we are further strained by an inward uneasiness, because we have hints that there is a way of life vastly richer and deeper than all of this hurried existence, a life of hurried serenity and peace and power."

The Bible tells us that the primary way to enter a life "richer and deeper" is by keeping the Sabbath. By keeping the Sabbath we set aside time to rest our bodies, pray to God, and express gratitude for our blessings. The unfortunate truth of our hurried existence is that we do not do a good job of setting this time aside. For some, Sabbath time seems old-fashioned. We think we have "too many important things" to be engaged in to stop and honor God. For others, doing nothing might seem like a waste, an inefficient way to spend our time.

When we explore the meaning and history of Sabbath we discover that keeping Sabbath is not about doing "nothing." Sabbath keeping is actually an active process that leads to a "richer and deeper" life, whether on Sundays or other times during the week.

This summer I invite you, even challenge you, to keep Sabbath time. Maybe your Sabbath will be Sundays. Or, maybe it can only be a few hours another day of the week. The key is to not make it too complicated. Rest, pray, give thanks, and read something that stirs your soul. I would like to leave you with a poem by Mary Oliver that illustrates a spiritual movement of learning and keeping the Sabbath. It's a poem that starts where many of us are -- in a restless state. But what I love about this poem is that it is aspirational and hopeful. It's called, appropriately, "Coming to God: First Days."

"Lord, what shall I do that I
Can't quiet myself?
Here is the bread, and
Here is the cup, and
I can't quiet myself.

To enter the language of transformation!
To learn the importance of stillness,
With one's hands folded!

When will my eyes of rejoicing turn peaceful?
When will my joyful feet grow still?
When will my heart stop its prancing
As over the summer grass?

Lord, I would run for you, loving the miles for your sake.
I would climb the highest tree
To be that much closer.

Lord, I will also learn to kneel down
Into the world of the invisible,
The inscrutable and the everlasting.
Then I will move no more than the leaves of a tree
On a day of no wind,
Bathed in light,
Like the wanderer who has come at last,
And kneels in peace, done with all unnecessary things:
Even motion, even words."

May this be a prayer for each of us this summer as we seek to break new ground in our life with God and with each other. There is hope for all of us!

With love and prayers,
Chip

Summer often affords us the time to think about our lives. Where are we going? What's becoming of the lives that we are living? What is the quality of the relationships that we value the most? Often we move so fast we fail to "check-in" and ask these important questions of ourselves.

Years ago I read something written by the author Sam Keen that captured my attention. It had to do with the issue of alignment. Alignment is the art of investing our time, effort, and love in the things that matter most. It is easy to fool ourselves and say one thing but do another. At times, we may even think that just because we're thinking good thoughts we're actually doing them. Real growth happens though when our time and focus is properly aligned with who and what we love.

I want to share with you a quote from Sam Keen. Though it is targeted towards issues of work and family, it can be translated into any aspect of life. I pray that we can all profit from his experience and wisdom:

"In working so much have I done violence to my being? How often, doing work that is good, have I betrayed what is better in myself and abandoned what is best for those I love? How many hours would have been better spent walking in silence in the woods or wrestling with my children?"

"Two decades ago, near the end of what was a good but troubled marriage, my wife asked me: 'Would you be willing to be less efficient?' The question haunts me."

Alignment. Investing in what matters most. Saying, believing and doing what we know is most important. May this summer be a fruitful time for you; a time of thinking, healing and transformation.

Love and Prayers,
Chip

At our 5:00 p.m. service this Sunday, we worshiped together with a liturgy designed for Labor Day. The Epistle was from Paul's first letter to the Corinthians, 1 Corinthians 3:10-14, and spoke of Jesus Christ as our foundation:

"According to the grace of God given to me, like a skilled master builder I laid a foundation, and someone else is building on it. Each builder must choose with care how to build on it. For no one can lay any foundation other than the one that has been laid; that foundation is Jesus Christ. Now if anyone builds on the foundation with gold, silver, precious stones, wood, hay, straw -- the work of each builder will become visible, for the Day will disclose it, because it will be revealed with fire, and the fire will test what sort of work each has done. If what has been built on the foundation survives, the builder will receive a reward."

The challenge Paul sets before us as we enter another year of labor is making sure that we are **using** Christ as our foundation in all that we do. Our challenge is to take the mundane and ordinary tasks of our lives and make them holy.

As Paul says, it does not matter whether we build on Christ's foundation with the extravagant (gold, silver, precious stones) or with the mundane and ordinary parts of life (wood, hay, straw). What matters is that we build on Christ. Our extraordinary and our mundane tasks must continue to be accomplished but we have the choice of how and why we choose to continue. We can choose who we serve with our actions.

No matter what we are doing in our day-to-day lives, Christ is available for us. If we are working, we can root our work in Christ. If we are playing, we can set our joy in Christ. If we are hurting, mourning, or weeping, we can anchor our pain in Christ. If we are sleeping, we can seek our rest in Christ. Christ is available to be the foundation of our whole life and if we allow Christ to strengthen us and to be our steady foundation in all that we do then we are setting our lives apart to be holy.

John

Today, September 14, is Holy Cross Day, a great feast day in the life of the Church that celebrates "the Cross" and all the meaning it contains. It would be impossible to ever comprehend all that the crucifixion means, but the most important thing is that it always holds relevant, powerful meaning for each of us if we pay attention. Right now for me, the cross is the amazing, sure sign that God is with us in our country as we seek to try to support one another through the disaster of Katrina. Here is a story to illustrate my point:

A grandfather found his grandson in his playpen screaming and crying at the top of his lungs. When little Bill saw his grandfather, he reached out his arms frantically and cried, "Out, Gampy, out! Up, Gampy, up!" Just as the old man reached down to pick up Bill, his daughter stepped in and said, "No, Dad, don't do that. Bill, you are not to get out of that pen. You are being punished, and you must stay in." Bill cried and cried, and his grandfather was deeply distressed by the tears of the child, but he didn't want to disrespect his daughter. Finally he found a solution. The old man climbed into the playpen and sat down with Bill, and the boy calmed right down.

The cross is all about God in Christ coming into this world and climbing into every situation we may find ourselves in. The cross is the sign of Christ's presence with us in any and all suffering, pain, and death. And beyond the cross there is the sign of the empty tomb -- new life. Christ is now in us as the hope of glory for all the world, and right now, especially, for all whose lives are devastated by Katrina. Let's be Christ-like in whatever way we can and be with them as the crucified Lord chose to be with us.

The Rev. Marty Hedgpeth

The day **after** an election is for me a defining moment for any country. I think I can say with confidence that none of us who voted in this year's election woke up to find that every person we voted for won. At least one of our candidates lost. And here is what makes me proud of our nation: though divided for months about who should be elected to public office, we stand united again today. We are united in our respect for the democratic process. We are united in our hopes that our newly elected officials can lead this country through very challenging times into greater opportunity, security, justice and peace for all. And as the great-granddaughter of a slave-owner, I trust we are also united in appreciating the historic, even spiritual, significance of the election of an African-American to the presidency.

Recently I heard someone ask our President-Elect, Barack Obama, why he actually wanted the job of president, considering the state of our nation. Obama replied that now is a great time to serve in public office because now there is an even greater opportunity to make an impact.

Likewise now is a great time to be the Church. The Church's message of Christ's hope, forgiveness and redemption shines brightest in times of uncertainty and loss. We have a powerful message to proclaim, but, more important, we have a powerful and loving God to lead us, strengthen us, challenge us, and care for us. We have a responsibility to share God's Spirit and message, to be a beacon of hope for one another and for our community and world.

I leave you with this portion of Psalm 16:

"O LORD, you are my portion and my cup;
it is you who uphold my lot.
My boundaries enclose a pleasant land;
indeed, I have a goodly heritage.
I will bless the LORD who gives me counsel;
my heart teaches me, night after night.

My heart, therefore, is glad, and my spirit rejoices;
my body also shall rest in hope.
You will show me the path of life;
in your presence there is fullness of joy,
and in your right hand are pleasures for evermore."

The Rev. Lisa Saunders

My mom sends me clippings from The New York Times every day. She sends a variety of articles that she thinks I'm interested in or should be interested in. It is a wonderful gift from her and a good array of stories, photos, and information that I love receiving.

Not long ago, when the economic meltdown was just erupting, I pulled from the envelope an ad from Harry Winston that said, "Cue the harps" right above a photo of a $25,000 "cushion-cut diamond in a micropave setting." I couldn't fathom why Mom sent this until I turned it over and saw another ad, exactly the same size, from Tiffany, which said, "There Are Times: to hold open a door, to surrender your seat, to thank someone in writing, to let bygones be gone, to remember your parents, to listen with care, to surprise with a gift, to mind your table manners, to honor tradition, to give voice to your heart."

That two famous jewelry stores could have exactly opposite messages reflects something of the choices we have in life, which our faith points out again and again -- life or death; light or darkness; hope or despair; faith or fear. Our good God will not choose for us, but has given us a clear hint of what is good in the sacrificial life-giving of Jesus. What do we choose and what do we teach our children to choose?

May this Thanksgiving be a time that we choose life and light and hope and faith (and all those simple yet meaningful things Tiffany proposes). May it be a time we give voice to our hearts and thank God for our abundant blessings.

The Rev. Marty Hedgpeth

In October, for the first time in 23 years of ministry, I officiated at a wedding that was not in a church. It was in Santa Fe in the garden at the home of the bride's parents. It was a beautiful walled garden, the rowan trees were laden with bright red berries, fall flowers were in bloom, pumpkins had been placed in perfect spots, a tiny water fountain gurgled in the background, and a clear turquoise New Mexico sky was like a canopy enveloping us. There were only 30 people there -- all very close family and friends. It was 5:30 p.m. so the sun was casting its last golden rays of light through the trees, illuminating corners that would soon be dark. It was one of the holiest weddings I have ever experienced.

When describing it all to Janice Brady, our Christian Education secretary and a devoted expert on Native American culture, she said that for Native Americans, that time of day -- when daylight just gives way to early evening -- is a very sacred time. I said, "Oh, you mean it's a thin time," equating this idea with the Celtic idea of thin places -- those places where the separation between this world and eternity is so "thin" that one can truly see and feel the presence of the divine, the atmosphere of heaven.

Advent is a time of year when we get far too busy and there seems far too little time in which to get everything done. It is a time when we tend to be at home either recovering from a Thanksgiving trip or preparing for a Christmas trip. We may not find ourselves in thin places, but we can find thin time. It may be different for each of us, but I suggest that we each find a time of day when we can be alone and still and silent. And in that moment, listen for the still, small voice of God. The prophets heard it, Mary heard it, even Joseph heard it. We can, too. Find a thin time in your day, and you will find Christ in you, the hope of glory.

The Rev. Marty Hedgpeth

Every year I get numerous people asking, "Why can't we sing Christmas carols now?" And each year I give the same answer, "It's not Christmas. It's Advent. We're very busy preparing for Christmas and all that preparation is important." Most are less than impressed with my answer, so let me try another one.

When I was about seven or eight years old, I was obsessed with my desire and need for roller skates. I was desperate for roller skates. I couldn't wait to find out if my request had been met. One day while no adults were in the house I found a stash of wrapped gifts, including several that had a roller skate box shape to them. But I wasn't satisfied. So I took them all and locked myself in the bathroom and very carefully open them all to see what I was getting. Among other things, I found roller skates, which brought me more relief than joy. I carefully rewrapped the packages and returned them to their secret spot. On Christmas morning, I knew just what was in several boxes and I opened them without any hope and expectation. Once open, I felt like I had been cheated of Christmas.

God sent Jesus "in the fullness of time," which means at the right time, when the world was as ready as it could be. As Episcopalians, we believe that seasons are a particular length because they provide the right amount of time to prepare for the next season. Singing Christmas carols from All Saints Day through December (as some radio stations would have us do) tires us out before Christmas even arrives. The birth of God incarnate is so huge an event that we miss the meaning by unwrapping it too early. So don't cheat yourself of the incredible miracle of the season of Christmas by celebrating it too soon. Much of the meaning is truly in the waiting and expecting and preparing and hoping.

The Rev. Martha Hedgpeth

Advent is like...

The mute button on a television remote control. The season of Advent is intended to quiet, to have a muting effect on, the clamor of Christmas. While Advent carols will never catch on quite the way Christmas carols do, the music and message of Advent try their best to drown out the rush of an over-commercialized holiday and help us experience the hush of Christ's peace.

A speed bump. In most of the places you find speed bumps, they are there because people won't slow down of their own accord. Christmas more often makes us feel that we need to hurry, that in fact, we are already behind. Advent works like speed bumps, compelling us to do what we will not do on our own: slow down enough to recognize the presence and work of Christ in our midst.

A child trying to get her parent's attention. When my children were toddlers and they wanted to be sure they had my attention, they would place their hands on either side of my face and turn my face until I was looking at them eye to eye. Advent is about turning our face towards God, and being humbled and delighted to discover that God's attention is fully upon us.

Advent is an early Christmas gift. Open now and enjoy.

Lisa

I went and got a Christmas tree on Saturday. It was 75 degrees. By the time I had found one, gotten it home and in the stand, I was in a complete pool of sweat and in a very bah, humbug mood. This is the time of year when lots of things seek to destroy the spirit of the season. Often we do more complaining than celebrating. Overindulgence reigns in eating, drinking, socializing and spending.

There are two truths to hear about this. First, quite simply, we each can say no to the overindulgence. It is our choice to engage in it or not. Second, quite amazingly, **nothing** we do can destroy the real spirit of this season. Madeleine L'Engle wrote a beautiful book about the birth of Jesus appropriately called "The Glorious Impossible." We may think that society has desecrated the birth of our Lord and Savior, but if you try, you can discover holiness -- grace, love, generosity, good will, and joy -- even in the overcrowded malls, endless parties, family gatherings, and elegant feasts. As Phillips Brooks wrote, "How silently, how silently, the wondrous gift is given! So God imparts to human hearts the blessings of his heaven. No ear may hear his coming, but in this world of sin, where meek souls will receive him, still the dear Christ enters in."

Look and listen and taste and see the little annunciations of the Lord's presence that God gives regardless of our distractions. It would be nice to have a little chill in the air, but I must admit, after leaving on Saturday for some time, I returned home and was enveloped in the smell of evergreens. The glorious impossible happened to me. May it happen to you, too.

Marty

Merry Christmas or Happy Holidays or Seasons Greetings? This has become an issue that has elicited the most unflattering and totally Godless attitudes of people of all faiths or non-faiths. I can't speak for others, but I will dare to speak for Christians. We need to be unapologetic and clear about what this time of year means for us. It is about the birth of Jesus, our Savior and Lord. Saying Merry Christmas should be our joyful, natural greeting. It is a way of offering the gift of Jesus to others, but also reminding us of the reason for the season. How many of us are caught up in consuming, traveling, partying, and decorating?

Yet even as we use a specifically Christian greeting, we are called to be Christ-like in our lives. I have been saddened to see and hear Christians bullying others who for good and not so good reasons don't want to be greeted in the name of Christ. Whenever someone acts like a bully, I wonder what he or she is afraid of. Christmas will still be Christmas for Christians centered in their faith. Christ was born long ago, and he is born here and now, again and again in the hearts and lives of individuals, regardless of what we say. The good news is that our God became incarnate in a tiny, powerless, dependent infant in a stable in the dark. It was the beginning of a clear word from God that real power is in powerlessness, that real receiving is in giving, that real gaining of self is in denial of self.

In this holiday season, remember the words of the angel to Mary and to the shepherds, "Don't be afraid." Don't be afraid to say Merry Christmas and don't be afraid if others choose not to. Remember the words of Paul, who described "a more excellent way" saying, "Love is patient; love is kind; love is not envious or boastful or arrogant or rude. It does not insist on its own way... It bears all things, believes all things, hopes all things, endures all things. Love never ends."

Love came down at Christmas in Jesus Christ. May our lives reflect that love no matter what our greeting. In the true spirit of the holiday and the season, I wish you all a very merry, happy, and holy Christmas.

The Rev. Marty Hedgpeth

What do you REALLY want for Christmas?

How long has it been since you seriously hoped that your wildest Christmas dreams would come true? How long has it been since Santa delivered the one thing you most hoped for even though you had hardly whispered your hope to anyone? What do you think the chances are for your Christmas wish to come true this year? I think you ought to dream the biggest dream you can and absolutely count on it coming true.

Pause to think about that biggest dream...no, not that one. A new car would be nice but it's not really your biggest dream. Dream bigger. Dream from the depths of your soul where your deepest dreams form in the presence of your deepest needs and fears. Is your dream a job? A home? Security? Health? Retirement? Forgiveness? A family? Love?

It is hard to be honest with yourself when your deepest needs and your deepest fears are involved. Being honest makes us vulnerable. Dreams and needs seem to suggest that we want something outside of ourselves and that means depending on someone other than ourselves. Many of us are afraid of depending on others because we don't want to be let down. We want to guard our secret needs and our true feelings instead of hoping that they might be realized.

Instead of guarding your dreams this year, join me in imagining that they will come true this Christmas. Join me in imagining that all of your needs will be provided for. Join me as I try to be childlike in my astonishment as I realize that Jesus is my greatest dream and fills my every need. May we all see that Jesus gives us a home, security, health, healing, forgiveness, family, love, a huge load of work to do in our job as Christians and the best retirement plan ever conceived of. May we each truly know and feel this year, more than ever, that our Christmas dreams really have come true!

Merry Christmas!
The Rev. John Porter-Acee

During this season of longing and waiting for Christ to be born anew into our lives and into our world, we are vulnerable to falling into the hustle and the bustle of consumerism. With the times we are all living through right now, I wonder how many people might feel like they are being crushed by the "weight of the world" this Advent. I also wonder how often we think critically about "the weight of the world" as it appears in our life and realize that most of the weight really is of the world. More often than not, the things that weigh us down in our lives are temporary, earthly problems.

Many times our worries revolve around things that we don't need but simply the things in life that we have convinced ourselves will make us more comfortable, happier or better in some way. The weight gets even heavier as we begin to fear the loss of things we "deserve" or are "entitled to." As with most of the dilemmas in our lives, Jesus offers us another option. Jesus offers us the freedom from the "weights" of the world if we chose to follow him. Jesus tells us that his "yoke is easy" and his "burden is light" (Matthew 11:30).

This year when the presents under the tree will not be as plentiful or as nice as years past, or the renovation that we promised for the coming year will not happen after all, or even if your family is faced with an unwanted move; remember that the peace you long for is not found in those places. The peace we seek is found when we are able to loose ourselves from the weights of the world and allow ourselves to claim the freedom that is available to us in Jesus.

When we pull the plow of love and service we will not tire. When we set our hearts on leveling the road for others, we will find that we stumble ever so rarely. When we sweat the sweat of a servant of the Lord we find we are showered in gifts that we could never deserve or be entitled to, and we feel as though we could fly in the absence of the weight we once knew in this world.

The Rev. John Porter-Acee

One of the benchmarks of adulthood is the first Christmas when you are more excited about a gift you are giving than about a gift you may be receiving. I remember well my first Christmas after college, and I was most excited about the gifts I had picked out, purchased and wrapped on a limited budget. I felt very grown-up and gave not a thought to what gifts I might receive. I knew my husband, Tim, had not had any time to shop, but it really didn't matter to me. He was a hospital intern, and shopping was not a high priority for my sleep-deprived, over-worked husband. In fact, he even had to work December 24, so I spent Christmas Eve alone that first year we were married. He was working 24 hour shifts in the emergency room and due to come off duty at 8:00 a.m. Christmas Day. I picked him up at the hospital with the car packed for the seven hour drive to our hometown. Tim climbed into the backseat of the car and slept the first few hours of the drive. I was excited and eager to get home, singing along to Christmas carols on the radio.

It began to snow as I drove, and by the time Tim awakened, the ground was covered in white. He crawled up to the front seat beside me, and we wondered together about when we had last seen a white Christmas and when we might see another. Then Tim pulled out of his green scrub suit pocket a piece of paper folded several times. He carefully unfolded the paper and held it up for me to see. It was a paper snowflake, like the kind a kindergartner makes cutting holes in a folded paper. But instead of using scissors, Tim had used a scalpel to cut the paper. The snowflake was a circle and all along the edges, he had meticulously cut out "I Love Lisa" over and over again. The snowflake had designs of intricate flowers and hearts that no pair of scissors could have accomplished. As you can imagine, I was delighted with Tim's gift, and for many Christmases to follow, that snowflake hung in a place of honor on our Christmas tree until it became so fragile and yellowed, I had to keep it in a safe, dry place if it was to last.

These weeks, and now days, before Christmas are not only about making preparations to give, but about knowing ourselves as the receivers we essentially are. No matter who we are, we stand at the manger empty-handed like the poor, hapless shepherds, acknowledging our emptiness next to the glory of God. It is a mark of maturity to take great pleasure in giving gifts to others, but we are all children at Christmas, blessed to receive the gift of God's great love for us.

In Christ,

The Rev. Lisa Saunders

"As far as the eye of God could see
Darkness covered everything.
Blacker than a hundred midnights
Down in a cypress swamp.
Then God smiled and the Light broke."

So James Weldon Johnson describes creation.

Then it happened all over again at Christmas when God smiled once more -- and the Light came on. And nothing we have done has ever been able to put that light out, although we have been endlessly creative in learning how to hide it behind clouds of our making.

God smiled and creation happened. God smiled at Bethlehem and all heaven broke loose as creation was renewed, refilled with promise and hope. And God is still smiling.

Of all the tales ever told, none has the power of Christmas to awaken hope, to lift the heart, to rekindle love, to make the spirit dance and sing. Christmas has withstood all the cynicism, the glitz, and the trivia with which we encrust it. The holy night still evokes the best from us, often despite our efforts to domesticate and control it, because the power of God's love perfectly revealed in the utter mystery of the holy child's birth transcends our drive to place the mystery in a context we can control.

The story of the night when all creation paused in its careening to witness the coming of the Creator into the middle of his creation is the stuff of our poetry, the province of our art, not because it is simply poetry or art, but because these are the languages we have for making stabs at mastering that which forever lies beyond our mastery. No event has evoked the magnificent and equally trivial responses that the birth in Bethlehem's mean stable has.

The music, the light that cuts through the soul's long, dark nights, the season's sights and sounds, the promise of companionship in our worship, all combine to lift spirits too often battered by the living of our days.

The mystery of the birth of Jesus transcends all we say about it, all that with which we surround it. It transforms our disappointments by transforming us from those who insist on action and results now to those who are learning, slowly and imperfectly, to live on the basis of the season's hope. The mystery of Christmas lies behind and beyond the ways we have devised for speaking about it, for it is the mystery of God's continuing love for his troubled, perplexed creation, love that keeps promising us the newness that is at the heart of the birth we celebrate.

For just as Jesus was in Bethlehem cradled in the most unlikely of places, so too is he now once again cradled in unlikely ways in us, in our will to embrace life and live it richly, to live it as ones who know that love will cast out fear, that all the darknesses will give way to the light that is the hope and the promise of Christmas.

Reach for the light and you will find that it has already wrapped you in its loving, transforming power. God will again smile and you will be made new as creation has been made new in the holy child.

God bless you now and every day of your life and forever.

Nick White

In the Episcopal Church we all have a good laugh at ourselves every year during Advent. We know that our denomination stands in contrast to the commercial world in between Thanksgiving and Christmas, and with a bit of a chuckle, we take comfort in being the oddballs this time of year. We don't sing Christmas carols, we don't decorate, we don't have big Christmas parties (at least **at** the church) and we try to focus on the season of Advent as being a season of preparation more than celebration. None of this is to say that we are "doing it right" or that anyone else is "doing it wrong" it is just a reminder of who we are.

As you jump in your cars today and notice that all of the Christmas music is off the radio, as you drive past the Christmas trees that are already on the street, and as the lights on the houses are taken down or at least no longer lit, continue to remember who we are. We are a people that believe that Christmas is much too big to be celebrated for just one day. If you didn't celebrate it before the 25th you better keep celebrating it now. We are a people that believe this season commemorates an event that changed our lives and our understanding of God forever. If our lives have not finished molding to this new understanding, we better keep molding them now. We are a people who learned from one child who came into this world that we must care about **every** child that comes into this world. If there are still any children without homes, then we must go and build them.

Merry Christmas,
John M. Porter-Acee III

It is still Christmas. One of the events in parish life that always shines with the meaning of this season is the Christmas Pageant. This year, as in some years past, there was a "problem" with the baby Jesus. Perhaps the baby got too squirmy or perhaps the baby became just too heavy for Mary, but as time went on the baby's head lopped over Mary's arm and slowly the tiny body slipped lower and lower in Mary's lap. Finally the baby's mother discreetly went onstage, took the child and gave Mary a doll to hold. A few years ago, the "problem" was a very disgruntled Jesus whose father finally snuck up onstage and simply knelt behind the Holy Family calming his child for the rest of the pageant.

It is a very human moment, but one that illustrates what Christmas is all about. Like those vigilant parents who see their children in distress or in danger and respond by going to them, so God in Christ has seen our brokenness and pain and has come and does come to us. Christ is here right beside us, not to obliterate the darkness, but to shine a light in the midst of darkness and to give us hope and a way through the darkness.

Are we aware of his presence? Do we seek him like the shepherds and magi? In the pageant, it is wonderful to see the children straining in the blinding spotlights to find their families in the crowd. And upon seeing them, the children break character, beam with joy and wave with abandon. Look for Christ in your life and when you find him, may you be filled with childlike joy and gladness.

The Rev. Marty Hedgpeth

Grief, Pain and Loss

Last fall I officiated at a funeral which included interring the ashes of the deceased in our Memorial Garden. I never noticed, but the family couldn't wait to tell me after the fact about what they saw. As I prepared to put the ashes in the ground, a butterfly landed on the bush right next to me, then it flew around me several times; and as I finished covering the burial spot, the butterfly flew off into the sky. For that family, resurrection was real because of the little sign of that butterfly.

A few weeks ago, when we had that long spell of unusually hot weather, I decided to put out my hummingbird feeder, despite the fact that I never get hummingbirds before May. It looked like that would be the case this year as well. But very early Easter morning as I got ready to come to church, I glanced out and then did a double and then a triple take -- there was a hummingbird on my feeder! In Native American tradition, the hummingbird is a symbol of the resurrection. For me, resurrection was real because of the little sign of that first hummingbird.

If the resurrection of Jesus is to be meaningful in our lives, we need to practice finding and rejoicing in little moments of resurrection in our everyday lives. Forgiveness is real and a relationship is restored; a child who was "lost" is "found"; an answer to prayer is discerned; hope rises in the midst of darkness; a butterfly or a hummingbird graces us with its presence. Little moments add up in such a way that we can say with profound faith and joy, Christ is risen; the Lord is risen indeed. Alleluia.

The Rev. Marty Hedgpeth

Our new vision for Christ Church is about building a spiritual home. For me, a spiritual home is a place where there are people who can, and want to, help carry your burdens. That's part of what we do when we pray for one another; we help shoulder another's pain or grief or worry or fear. I trust that when we pray for others, we help to lighten or make bearable whatever weighs down their hearts, minds and spirits. It's not that misery loves company, but that there is comfort in knowing we are not alone in our suffering; there is relief and strength given when we know someone genuinely cares and seeks to understand and lessen our burden, even when it is a burden that cannot be taken away. Too often we think of prayer as a lever to move God, but it is a lever that can lift us, and those for whom we pray, closer to God's life-giving hope and power to make all things new.

The Swedish statesman, Daq Hammeraskjold said "What makes loneliness an anguish is not that I have no one to share my burden, but this: I have only my own burden to bear." Hammeraskjold's remarks point to a divine mystery: It is lovely to have someone help shoulder our burdens, but ahh, it is lovelier even still to help shoulder someone else's burden.

I'm not generally a biblical literalist, but Paul's challenge to the Galations (Galatians 6:2), "Bear one another's burdens and in this way you will fulfill the law of Christ," I take at his word.

Lisa+

Verdery Kerr delivered a very important sermon in the Contemporary Service on Sunday, November the 18. He dared to enter a place where we might try to examine our suffering and find the gift of light and life. Verdery compared our seasons of suffering to the seasons in the natural world and found bitter times to be just as important to our growth as the pruning seasons are for the earth. He challenged us in this season of Thanksgiving to consider giving thanks **even** for our struggles and our pains. I invite you to take on Verdery's challenge this year with the help of Psalm 139:

7Where can I go from your spirit?
    Or where can I flee from your presence?
8If I ascend to heaven, you are there;
    if I make my bed in Sheol, you are there.
9If I take the wings of the morning
    and settle at the farthest limits of the sea,
10even there your hand shall lead me,
    and your right hand shall hold me fast.
11If I say, 'Surely the darkness shall cover me,
    and the light around me become night',
12even the darkness is not dark to you;
    the night is as bright as the day,
    for darkness is as light to you.

Though God does not cause the pain in our lives God is there in the midst of our pain. God is **always** with us and where God is there is always thanks to be given. Holidays are often the hardest times to give thanks for the great tragedies or pains in our life. The final words of Psalm 139 given here invite you to have faith in our God who bears all of our pain without falter. God's plan to make all things whole is not thwarted by cancer or disease. God cannot be stopped by death or drunkenness. God can bring the blessing of his light into your darkest night. Give thanks for all of the places that you may find God. Give thanks **even** for our struggles and pains.

John M. Porter-Acee III

I bought a book a few years ago that I am finally sitting down to read. The title of the book both attracted and repelled me. It's titled "Toward Holy Ground: Spiritual Directions for the Second Half of Life" by Margaret Guenther. Margaret is an Episcopal priest, who has been the director of the spiritual direction center at General Seminary in New York City.

I bought the book when I observed that most of my childhood dreams and hopes didn't take me past age 40. I didn't dream past 40. I couldn't fathom being past 40. I guess I didn't think anything much new happened after 40. Now I'm closer to 50, and it's past time to read Guenther's book.

One of the first things she writes catches me by surprise. She writes that the second half of life is the age of the amateur. I would have thought just the opposite. It would seem that the first half of life is spent honing skills and talents so that the second half of life is spent as a professional: skillful, capable, responsible, proficient in whatever work, at home or out of the home, you do.

Guenther describes amateurs as "lovers, drawn to their work and their commitments by love, not duty, sustained by the gift of joy and wonder in all God's works." What a wonderful outlook on what could be the driving force in the second half of our lives! Many of us cannot change our professions, but often what first attracted us to our job is not always what sustains and nourishes us in our work. Relationships at work, or the fact that our work provides for loved ones at home, may offer us more fulfillment than the mechanics of what we do. The doctor who entered medicine to cure people discovers that comforting and accompanying people on difficult journeys brings the greatest satisfaction. A banker finds greater pleasure mentoring new employees than bettering the bottom line. A mother learns that teaching herself to paint is as joyful as helping a child to finger-paint.

I write this on the day of the NBA draft, when so many amateur ballplayers become professionals. Wouldn't it be fun if there were a reverse draft for anyone over 40 who wants to go from professional to amateur status? Guenther says it can happen anyway as love, not duty, becomes our greatest commitment in all we do.

The Rev. Lisa Saunders

Once a little girl was sent on an errand by her mother. She took much too long in returning home. Her mother demanded an explanation when the child got home. The little girl explained that on her way she had met a friend who was crying because she had broken her doll. "Oh, so you stopped to help her fix her doll," said the mother. "No," replied the child, "I stopped to help her cry."

Our natural human instincts are like those of the mother in this story. When things are wrong, we want to fix them. We want to be about doing and repairing and creating results. And that is usually a very good thing. But as Christians we are called to know that there are times when the best thing to do is not fix things, but to simply be present with another, to share in suffering and thereby ease the burden, though without results.

Sometimes this ministry of "presence" is more difficult then a ministry of "doing things." But I have found that when I have been able to be still and simply be with someone, it has helped the other person and it has also deepened my level of compassion.

In a life of faith, Jesus applauds those who do what they can. Sometimes that means fixing things. Other times that means simply being with another person in their situation.

Marty

The best parables disturb us, meddle in our business, and send us off reconfiguring stuff we thought we already had figured out. Therefore, I'd have to say that Hurricane Katrina has us all living deep inside a parable. It's definitely disturbing, meddlesome and has a bunch of folks trying to figure out what went wrong with our previous figuring. Of course, for thousands of Americans, Hurricane Katrina was more than parabolic; it was deadly; it was destructive; it was devastating.

Another hurricane is barreling toward landfall as you read this, threatening to strike areas where Katrina evacuees have taken shelter. Coincidental? Providential? Unlucky? Or pointedly instructive? Likely some folks are wondering if God is angry with us, trying to teach us some cosmic lesson. I think God is always trying to teach us some cosmic lesson, but I do not believe God is making these hurricanes like a youngster makes snowballs to throw on a wintry day. I do believe God created a world in which hurricanes are a possibility, as are gentle rains and beautiful sunsets. Natural disasters occur because nature is allowed to behave in accordance with its nature. There is an independence given to all creation, for as physicist and priest John Polkinghorne writes, "God has brought into being a world which he allows to be itself and to make itself."

What humanity "makes" of this disaster is where our attention should be paid. Jesus taught us that acts of love, compassion, justice and healing bring blessing to the world. Certainly the travesty and horror of Hurricane Katrina, September 11th, and every tragedy in history (and in each of our personal histories) has found reconciliation, hope and new life only when people reach out to help, respect and listen to one another -- never asking if such attention, sacrifice and expense are deserved or are fair. The parables Jesus told often serve to remind us that our blessings mean nothing if they do not compel us to be a blessing to others. Maybe living inside the parable Hurricane Katrina provides can do the same.

The Rev. Lisa Saunders

"Knowing that suffering produces endurance, and endurance produces character, and character produces hope, and hope does not disappoint us, because God's love has been poured into our hearts through the Holy Spirit...." (Romans 5:3-5)

"Reality can be harsh...you shut your eyes to it only at your peril because if you do not face up to the enemy in all his dark power, then the enemy will come up from behind some dark day and destroy you...." (Frederick Buechner)

When my brother was 21, a university infirmary doctor told him if he continued living the way he was living, he would be dead in two years. More than three decades later, after a circuitous path comprised of short stints of health and extended periods of self-destruction, he's one of my heroes. He's an incarnation of Paul's declaration above and Buechner's statement. After spiraling downward it seems like forever, now he has moments like one last month when alone on a Montana mountaintop, he knelt, overcome with sheer joy and thanksgiving for his life and for abundant goodness in this world. He prays often and long for those who have wounded him. This transformation didn't come cheap. There has been and continues to be hard work. He didn't and doesn't do this by himself. There is the Lord...mostly indirectly through friends, family members and strangers. I venture he's healthier in mind, body and soul than his three siblings. Finally, he's essentially himself, as created by God. He's no pristine angel. He's still stubborn, drives too fast, etc...Yet there is a clear call he honors. Beyond his profession, he's front-and-center for others engaged in various life-and-death struggles hinted by these quotes. It was grace to be around him last week during a family vacation. I reminded him often that I was the holy, good son and he was still the black sheep, bad son!

My brother's journey is not exceptional. I know these words from Romans and Buechner to be true. In recent months I have been privileged with conversations with numbers of parishioners thrust at points in their lives into some darkness professional or personal.

The Blessing of a Ginkgo Tree 133

In this world or the next, they too have gone or are on the way of suffering-endurance-character-hope. Christ Church is highly fertilized with human miracles and transformations. However we look on the outside, there are a multitude of such heroes and heroines among us. In every instance I know, they did not do this alone. Our congregation continues to be blessed with hardships undergone and grace received.

In Christ,
Verdery

How do you get to Carnegie Hall? When I began piano lessons in my 40s I truly learned that the way is practice, practice, practice. In a Sports Illustrated profile, the great New England quarterback Tom Brady claimed that his favorite part of football is practice, because that's when real learning and growth takes place.

We are great advocates of practice and training when it comes to music, sports, and many other life skills, but curiously we expect to simply have faith. It took the recent, tragic deaths of young Amish girls, shot at their schoolhouse in Lancaster County, Pennsylvania, and the astonishing forgiveness exhibited by their families to reveal that a meaningful, living faith depends on practice. Beginning as toddlers, the Amish learn strict gospel guidelines that they follow through a lifetime of practice. The extraordinary forgiveness they have incarnated in these dark days was possible because of years of forgiving small things, questionable things, trivial things, and hard things.

The deaths of those little girls may be slightly redeemed by our commitment to practice our faith. Practice forgiveness. Practice servanthood. Practice generosity. Practice resurrection. The more we practice faith in little things, the more we will grow faithful enough to do extraordinary things.

The Rev. Martha H. Hedgpeth

This year God has made me more keenly aware of how painful this season can be for many of us, and I am grateful for the pastoral impact of our quiet and quieting observance of Advent. All around us, joy is issued as an imperative; yet for some, experiencing joy not only seems an impossibility but a betrayal. Losses magnify; hurt intensifies; loneliness deepens.

In times of difficulty, some people are quick to remark that "God never gives you more than you can handle" and in saying such, imagine that these are words of comfort. I am not comforted by the idea that God's help comes by means of being certain I remain one straw short of snapping beneath the weight of my burdens. I need a God who can do more than just hold back the last straw.

And I believe we have a God who can do more. Some of our burdens **are** lifted and taken away. Some are lightened when they are shared. And some of our burdens cannot be lifted or lightened, but they can be transformed by God's grace into privileges, into passions, into unexpected blessings, into thresholds of lives remade with surprising goodness. That is the hope and promise born to us at Christmas.

Be gentle and attentive to those you know, especially if it is yourself for whom this season rubs raw. And remember that God is well practiced in bringing forth new life in bleak mid-winters.

The Rev. Lisa Saunders

"I have always felt that failure is a completely underrated experience."*

I read that quote in a waiting room magazine recently. I scribbled it down, so I wouldn't forget it. The experience of failure, our own or that of someone we love or trust, is usually painful and disturbing. We feel lousy, and have trouble anticipating anything more but continued failure.

When Jesus sent his disciples off in pairs to preach, teach and heal, about the only instruction he gave them was what to do when they experienced failure. "Shake off the dust that is on your feet," he tells them when their message fails or they are rejected. Move on; don't wallow in failure or let it define you.

Failures often determine our course in life; they can thrust us in a different direction or raise our resolve and commitment to the one we are on. Failures teach us about hope and trust and resurrection. Failures remind us that God is always doing a new thing, and that God's mercies are new every morning. Failures increase our compassion and empathy for others. Failures keep us humble and aware that all grace is undeserved. Success has a much harder time instilling these lessons.

Jesus was an utter failure by the standards of his day -- executed as a penniless, friendless traitor. It is not always true, but sometimes what looks like failure is an avenue God uses to draw us closer to him, and to our truest selves.

Lisa

* AARP Magazine, an interview with the actor Kevin Costner. Surprised?

When I unfolded the newspaper and saw the headlines, my heart sank. An earthquake in Haiti! Of all places, Haiti! That little half-of-an-island country is already the poorest country in the hemisphere. This natural disaster seems even more disastrous.

When natural disasters strike, I still ask: How could God allow this to happen? An earthquake that size is always destructive, but in Haiti, there is already so much suffering and poverty, it seems cruel.

John Polkinghorne, a priest and physicist, has helped me think through these matters in the past, and I hear his voice again today. Natural disasters are not the punitive hand of God; they are the result of the independence God has bestowed upon creation.

I believe that God has chosen to infuse all of creation with some measure of freedom. Nothing in creation lives or operates only like a programmed robot. Even the smallest of cells has the freedom to mutate, which can result in things wondrous and beautiful, or tragic and horrific. If God blocked the consequences of evil human choices, like murder, and prevented natural disasters, like an earthquake, then moral responsibility would disappear and the natural order would become incoherent.

Events like earthquakes don't deny or refute God's loving care for this world, but often reveal it. As the possibilities for suffering are endless, so are the possibilities for goodness. Thank God the world is open to more variables than those prescribed by physics only.

In the Eucharistic prayer we use at the contemporary service, we pray that we might live lives of justice, love and prayer. For the sake of the people in Haiti, use your God-given freedom to make a difference for good.

Peace,
Lisa

I watched one of my favorite movies last weekend: "The Miracle Worker," a film adapted from Helen Keller's autobiography. In "The Story of My Life," Keller shares of her deep faith and remarkable vision of life, despite being blind and deaf. She wrote, "So much has been given to me, I have not time to ponder over that which has been denied."

When teaching people how to write their own autobiography, a professor of literature* suggests first telling your life story as a story of empowerment. Where did you learn that you counted for something and that what you do matters? Next she suggests telling your story as a story of loss. How has grief shaped you and altered your path? Then she says tell your life story as a story about grace. What unbidden and undeserved opportunities, gifts, reprieves, and relationships served as navigating stars?

In each of these ways of telling our story -- empowerment, loss and grace, I think we are being asked to trace the presence and work of God in our lives, to notice his great love for us and his transcendent power to make all things new. Perhaps we can see that best only when looking backwards. Whatever chapter of your life you are working on now, I hope you can see God at work in it, or at the very least, see evidence of his tools laying about.

I close with one more gem from Helen Keller: "Although the world is full of suffering, it is also full of the overcoming of it."

Lisa+

*Marilyn Chandler McEntyre, Professor of Literature at Westmont College in Santa Barbara

Every year I watch and wait for that certain week. It's never the same week each year. But it always comes, and it never disappoints. That week is here -- when the ginkgo tree that stands sentinel by the church doors turns a brilliant, buttery blush.

At the 5:00 service last Sunday, the tree smoldered under the late afternoon sun, and cast a warm, yellow shadow. It was this week several years ago that I took a picture of my daughter, Caroline, standing by the then much shorter tree, dressed in her Raggedy Ann Halloween costume. Twelve years ago, I took a handful of the yellow leaves with me when I went to New York to visit Mary and Tom Nicoll, a former associate rector here. It was my way of bringing some of the glory of Christ Church along with me.

I was never particularly good in science classes, but it seems to me that the changing of leaves has something to do with photosynthesis and the sun. I remember learning that photosynthesis causes the leaves to be green, and when it stops or slows, the leaves turn their natural color. Autumn reveals the tree's true colors. Of course, our ginkgo tree is beautiful in the summertime in all its abundant greenness, but this week in the fall, it reveals an even greater splendor.

There is a wonderful hymn, (#657) that includes this phrase:

"Changed from glory into glory,
'til in heaven we take our place,
'til we cast our crowns before thee,
lost in wonder, love and praise."

I trust that somehow, someway, I am and you are being "changed from glory into glory." God's handiwork is evident this week in the ginkgo tree, and I know that people, too, shine, even glow, when their truest, God-given colors are revealed. I think that such a revealing is the point of everything we do at church.

Ginkgo trees don't drop their leaves slowly, but all at once, such that in another week or so, a silky, yellow carpet will encircle its trunk. Take one of the leaves home with you. Let its beauty remind you of the glory and transformation God intends for each of us.

The Rev. Lisa Saunders

People will often ask me, if, in my line of work, it is depressing to be a part of so many funerals. In the past six weeks, I have taken part in five funerals. It is far more common for six weeks to pass in which I am not involved with any funeral. Certainly there is great sadness -- sometimes a crushing, elephantine sadness -- tied to death, and I can, by no means, sidestep it. Even when I do not know the person who has died, I feel its unyielding weight in the lives of those around me.

And yet, at any funeral it is my job and my honor, to proclaim the astounding, hopeful good news of the resurrection of the dead, and to commend the soul of one beloved to a God who loves and knows that soul the best. Our Episcopal liturgy for the burial of the dead is triumphant yet tender, solemn yet spirited.

It is enchanting for me to cradle a baby at baptism; it is stirring to stand with a couple as they make vows of marriage. However when officiating at a burial, more than feeling sad, I am deeply moved, and often freshly converted, by God's grace and pledge of hope given to us. As is written in our burial liturgy, "even at the grave we make our song, 'alleluia, alleluia, alleluia.'"

Next Wednesday, All Saints Day, we remember aloud by name all those saints who died in the last year who were members of our congregation or family members of our parishioners. Some folks also ask that names of loved ones who died in years past be included.

It is not depressing to be part of someone's entrance into eternal life. I consider it a holy privilege.

Lisa Saunders

Faith and Gratitude

Years ago I used to drive up a mountain to meet with an older Catholic priest who was known for great spiritual wisdom. On one visit I shared with him that I had many things going on in my life. He asked if I prayed. I told him that I did but that it was occasional at best. He instructed me, "Grace only lasts 24 hours." I told him I was puzzled, as I had been taught that God's grace was freely and abundantly given. How could it "expire" and last for only 24 hours? He then looked at me squarely and said, "You are missing the point. It doesn't expire; but your awareness that you need grace does. You must spend time with God each day to gain enough strength for today."

I have been doing quite a bit of listening these days to our parish and I am hearing many consistent themes in all of our lives. We are fearful. We are anxious. We are grieving. We feel powerless. It seems to me these feelings, though not desirable, are in fact normal for difficult economic times like these. Is there an opportunity we have this Lent to spend more time in prayer to remember God's provision and promise to "not abandon us" to comfort, guide, and direct us through the power of the Holy Spirit? If you are looking for a great read this Lent read "Making All Things New" by Henri Nouwen. I re-read it each Lent. In the book Nouwen writes:

"Jesus does not respond to our worry-filled way of living by saying that we should not be so busy with worldly affairs. He does not try to pull us away from the many events, activities, and people that make up our lives. He does not tell us that what we do is unimportant, valueless, or useless. Nor does he suggest that we should withdraw from our involvements and live quiet, restful lives removed from the struggles of the world. Jesus' response to our worry-filled lives is quite different. He asks us to shift the point of gravity, to relocate the center of our attention, to change our priorities. Jesus wants us to move from the 'many things' to the 'one necessary thing.'"

So what is that one thing? It's God in Jesus Christ. We connect with Him through prayer. One view of prayer is that it is a huge effort we make to hurl ourselves toward Him with hopes He will rescue us. Another view of prayer is that it is a way of becoming radically open to God's present grace that is available to those who are willing to take time to sit and be still and "know that I am God."

There is enough grace to bring us through the challenges we face. There always is. Take time this Lent to pray deeply -- wherever you are, whenever you can. Pray for "enough" at least every 24 hours. Become radically open to God's superabundant love and God will reach out to you in your openness to Him and give you "enough for today."

The Rev. Chip Edens

"Love your neighbor as you love yourself." (Matthew 22:34-40). As Christians, I believe that most of us feel a certain obligation to others. We know that Christ calls us to love one another. Whether we act on it or not, the countless, parables, sermons, and classes we have heard have pounded the moral value of helping others into our conscience. Have we overlooked Jesus' desire for us to love ourselves? Is it possible that we have never taken the time to think through the fact that Jesus equalizes the need for loving others with our need to love ourselves?

Last night my wife and I watched a program about Randy Pausch, the highly acclaimed author of "The Last Lecture," who lost his battle with cancer last Friday. In one of the interview clips Randy recounted that some of the best advice he had ever received came from a flight attendant: "Put on your own oxygen mask before you try to assist others." Randy did not take this advice as a simple instruction for flight safety, but rather something that we should take into all aspects of our life. Christ does call us outside of ourselves but we are none the less called within ourselves. If we are to serve others we must learn to serve ourselves well first. We are not able to even remove a speck out of someone else's eye if we do not first remove the plank out of our own eye. (Matthew 7: 3-5)

Where does the oxygen in your life come from? Is it prayer? Study? Exercise? Worship? Fellowship? Mission? Do you realize the importance of finding the breath of life? Have you thought about how you cannot reach your potential as a student, father, friend, wife, or worker if you do not have your own "mask" securely fastened? How can Christ Church help you breathe deeply from the breath of God?

May we all seek and find God's breath and in doing so equip ourselves with the potential God dreams for each of us.

The Rev. John Porter-Acee III

Today is the feast day of Evelyn Underhill. Born in 1876, she grew up in London as the only child of a barrister and his wife. Like any good Anglican, she was confirmed, but had no formal religious training. Yet she became one of the great spiritual writers of the 20th century.

She is one of my heroes of the faith because she was convinced that a deep life of prayer, a mystical life, is available to every person of faith, even you and me.

Prayer becomes meaningful in our lives only when we demystify it and make it a part of our everyday existence. It is in advocating this idea that Evelyn Underhill has helped me in my life of prayer. For today, let me give you a few Underhill nuggets that may strengthen you in your life of prayer.

On the beginning of a life of prayer:
"The spiritual life does not begin in an arrogant attempt at some peculiar kind of other-worldliness, a rejection of ordinary experience. It begins in the humble recognition that human beings can be very holy, full of God."

On the example of Jesus' early life of prayer:
"After the central mystery of Jesus' birth... We see the new life growing in secret. Nothing very startling happens. We see the child in the carpenter's workshop. He does not go outside the frame of the homely life in which He appeared. It did quite well for Him, and will do quite well for us; there is no need for peculiar conditions in order to grow in the spiritual life, for the presence of God's Spirit is present everywhere and at all times."

On a prayer life that is not self-serving:
"Christ was trained in a carpenter's shop; and we persist in preferring a confectioner's shop. But the energy of rescue, the outpouring of sacrificial love, which the [prayerful] life demands, is not to be got from a diet of devotional meringues and eclairs."

Prayer is the way we nurture our relationship with God. May the life and the words of Evelyn Underhill be an inspiration to us all to pray plainly, honestly, and often.

The Rev. Marty Hedgpeth

"With God All Things Are Possible." This phrase is found in the 19th chapter of the Gospel of Matthew. Jesus is speaking, to his disciples' astonishment, after confounding them yet again with unconventional thinking. Rather than viewing wealth and possessions as a blessing, Jesus has described them as a burden. His words recall for me the closing statement of an Ethiopian village chief to a parishioner-and-friend several years ago, "I will pray for you with your burden of affluence." Jesus declares that even things (think salty comedian George Carlin's STUFF) do not prevent God from acting and intervening in our lives.

Recently I've been thinking a lot not about the "burden of affluence," but rather the burdens of deficits and history many carry within. It is especially in these circumstances I hear Jesus: "**All things are possible with God**." When somewhere in childhood a person has not received what is due (affirmation, unqualified love, absolute embrace, value and worth), a hole within gets created. It can remain deeply set forever ... and can be filled with all sorts of bogus, counterfeit, destructive distractions/addictions. I've come to understand Paul's admonition in Ephesians about contending with "principalities and powers" to include a battle within many a man and woman. Engaging in such struggles is a noble, sacred, arduous venture.

Recently I was at a graduation dinner for two dozen men who had been in training with three more senior spiritual advisors for two years. These younger men had been chosen for leadership development in relationship with Christ. These three senior men stated that the foremost truth for the candidates to hear and accept is how absolutely and completely they are loved by the Lord. Elders were speaking to the next generation. Grown men addressing other men in love!

Christ Church is one of those places where this individual battle within continues to be entered; where all sorts of spiritual resources are marshaled communally: prayer, study, worship, and service. I find this place to be stunning, amazing, and transformational because of the collective impact of parishioners' honesty, courage, generosity and vulnerability. The combination of these and our spiritual disciplines make room for God to work miracles...for burdens and deficits to be lifted. I know firsthand here... **With God all things are possible.**

Blessings,
Verdery

I hadn't worn my raincoat in a while, and when I put it on yesterday, I was delighted to discover a twenty dollar bill in one of its pockets. I was reminded of being told once that "every day has a hundred pockets." In every day there is something precious, lovely and worthy to be kept. Some days are full of treasures; we practically trip over them they are so abundant. But other days, we have to look harder, longer and deeper to find any token of beauty or goodness to keep. Sometimes the only thing worth pocketing in a day is a clearer realization of our need for God.

The days of summer are intended to help us be better at filling our pockets with the treasures of each day. Summertime is supposed to offer us a slower pace where we might notice a bird dunking his head in a birdbath, a child's sunburned nose, wildflowers stubbornly in bloom by the road, the softness of the air at twilight, the familiar laughter of someone we love.

I hope it is easy for you to fill up today's hundred pockets. What we tuck away for safekeeping today might be important to hold tightly on our next rainy day.

Lisa+

Until recently, I found the depiction of Jesus' body on a cross to be unduly violent and gruesome. The representation of His physical body on a cross has a title of crucifix. I was much more at peace with an empty cross. Years ago though, I encountered an inkling of where I am now. After staying in a Roman Catholic Center, I noted that an empty cross made me nervous. It prompted me to wonder if somehow in my life I was supposed to be the guy on the cross!

This past June, an eight-day Ignatian discipline in a Jesuit House brought front-and-center the scene of a body hanging on a cross. Everywhere I went there were crucifixes. Wooden, ceramic, metal, etc.... Not a room in this large facility could be found without one. This core Christian icon began to grow on me.

Here's why. When I focus on a crucifix, it's clear to me what Jesus gave and how he lived. He chose not to allow anything to compromise His relationship with God, His values, His principles. In this world eternally beset with anxiety, story-lines of scarcity, angers, rage, lust for power, Jesus opted for an alternative existence characterized by joy and abundance. He did not pretend that evil, ugliness, and nastiness did not exist. Yet, pressures, threat of death, excruciating pain were not enough to entice Him to sully himself. Having submitted self to God, He gave his all. When I gaze upon a crucifix, I now see that this path is the way I aspire to live and die. With arms wide open to the good and bad this world can bring, not living defensively nor being insulated from assaults and onslaughts, I am called not to be safe and secure. While it's a long haul, it's the only way that makes any sense. Do I actually live this way? All too rarely. A crucifix reminds me, however, that the bar for my life is high. I know too that whatever my performance I remain loved and held dear. This doesn't take me "off the hook." Actually it inspires me to be more than I am, to partner with that body on the cross; for the world's sake, for God's sake and for my sake.

Blessings,
Verdery

I hope you have read (or will read) a remarkable book, "The Gift of Peace," the last words -- a testament really -- of Chicago's Cardinal Bernardin, who died in 1996. I hope it's still in print. It's a spellbinding document of faith, courage, wit, and wisdom.

You may know Cardinal Bernardin's story. In 1995, this true giant of the Christian faith was diagnosed with pancreatic cancer and given less than a year to live. He devoted all of his remaining time and energy to going about his ministry until just before his death. And he wrote an account of that last year, his thoughts about his life and his death.

He wrote the journal's last words on All Saints' Day, November 1st, 1996, and died thirteen days later. Using his last bit of energy, he wrote this at the very end of his testament:

"What I would like to leave behind is a simple prayer -- that each of you may find what I have found -- God's special gift to us all, the gift of peace, that same peace Christ carried into the room with his apostles. When we are at peace, we find the freedom to be most fully who we are, even in the worst of times. We let go of what is non-essential and embrace what is essential. We empty ourselves so that God may more fully work within us, and we become instruments in the hand of God."

Faithful stewardship of whatever you have and whatever you are is simply that: emptying self of self so that God can use you, can use me. The Church -- that is you and I -- is the chief agent on earth of this peace, for ourselves, for those we love, for the world always so in need of God's own peace that passes understanding.

I have told this story before, but it bears repeating. There was a three year old boy whose parents presented him with a new baby sister. Of course he was fascinated by this new little one, and wanted to poke and tickle her and wiggle her toes. One night not long after his sister had arrived, the boy tip-toed into her room where the parents, listening on the monitoring system, heard him say: "Tell me about God. I've almost forgotten."

Tell me about God. I've almost forgotten. The Christian life is a journey of return from the One from whom we have come and in whom, for the time being, we live and move and have our being. What part of God have you or I forgotten that makes us not understand the riveting necessity in our own lives of supporting God's work? What part about God, what characteristic of this loving God, have we forgotten, when we don't pay adequate attention?

Cardinal Bernardin speaks of the peace of God that he felt at the end of his life as he neared the end of his journey of return. He wanted himself and us to remember the God from whom we have come and towards whom we journey.

Question: Do you and I remember God and, if so, what do we intend to do about it?

See you in church. That's always a good step, for that's where we can discover that the gathered community of faith does a better job of remembering than we can do on our own.

Bless you all,
The Rev. Nick White

I was in Wal-Mart last week and watched a woman, with a baby on her hip and shopping bags in hand, insisting that her three-year-old follow her out of the store. He was much more fascinated by an array of bubble gum and candy dispensers and ignored his mother until she threatened, "If you don't come right now, I'm leaving without you." He turned and saw his mother half-way out the door and skedaddled after her. It's been a while since I've been in her shoes, but I remember wielding that same threat to my own defiant children. (These days, however, threatening to stay with my children is more effective.)

I was reminded of all of this when I read an email our bishop, Michael Curry, sent to the clergy and staff of the diocese. He wrote recommending a book for study in congregations entitled "The Rapture Exposed: The Message of Hope in the Book of Revelation," by Barbara R. Rossing. Dr. Rossing is Professor of New Testament at the Lutheran School of Theology. The book is a response to the popular "Left Behind" fiction bestsellers by Timothy LaHaye and Jerry Jenkins, which describe the Second Coming of Jesus Christ as a time of destruction, chaos, when some of us are taken up to heaven, and some of us are left behind to fend for ourselves in a world increasingly dominated by evil. Bishop Curry writes, "I do believe in the Second Coming. I believe that Jesus will come again, not to destroy the world but to heal it, not to perpetuate the old creation of violence and destruction but to establish the new creation of healing and peace. I believe that he shall come again with power and great glory." Both Curry and Dr. Rossing find the Left Behind series of books theologically dangerous, believing "God loves the world and will never leave the world behind." The Left Behind series seems to encourage faithfulness out of fear of being on the wrong side in a final battle. If you have ever read the Book of Revelation, (upon which the Left Behind books are said to be based), then you know it is ludicrous to suggest that the last book of the Bible offers a clear-cut, unambiguous timeline of the end of the world or the Second Coming. It is a highly interpretative vision that concludes with the triumph of the City of God in which God will wipe away every tear and all shall be made new.

You and I both know that the mother at Wal-Mart wasn't about to leave her three-year-old son behind, any more than I would have left any of my children behind when I used the same threat. We were just being manipulative to gain obedience. Some might agree God is doing the same because the stakes (our salvation) are high. Yet, the God Jesus reveals to me is compassionate, forgiving, and all about reconciliation and offering abundant life. Jesus shows me that God is the ultimate champion of no child left behind exactly because the stakes are high, and that it is not us, but our selfishness and pride, our fearfulness and envy, that need to be left behind.

The Rev. Lisa Saunders

My mom is a spectacular cook, so yesterday when she offered me a meatloaf from her freezer, I immediately accepted. Hers is the only meatloaf on the planet that I actually love. Then she said the dreaded words, "Let me know how you like it -- I tried a new recipe." Faster than the speed of light I transformed into a 5-year-old with a look of disgust on my face and asked what was in it and why did she do that? She didn't answer my questions, but said, "Well, if you don't want it, I'll keep it." To which I grudgingly responded with a sigh, "No, I'll take it and try it." My mom is such a good cook that I'm willing to give it a try.

As I was driving home with my mystery meatloaf, I began to laugh at myself and to see the connection between my response to my mother's change in a cherished dish and our response to change in the Church and in ways of understanding and expressing faith. We hate change and quote scripture accordingly: "Jesus Christ is the same yesterday and today and forever." (Heb. 13:8) But the point of this verse isn't that we should always keep everything the same; the point is that Jesus' work of forgiveness and love, his example of true humanity, his revelation of resurrection life will always stand fast in the midst of our changing lives and our ways of expressing those truths. The verse is an appeal to be open to change, not to reject it.

As in every parish I have known, change at Christ Church is first resisted, then grudgingly endured, then embraced, then considered the way it has always been. As we move through the coming weeks and months of change, let's be open to the new and wondrous ways that change can actually bring new life. Last Sunday, leaving the Contemporary Service, someone who would never, ever have chosen to attend, told me that she actually liked it! That's the kind of attitude Jesus calls us to have, that's the kind of attitude that fosters joy, hope, and expectation.

As for that meatloaf, I'll have to get back to you. It's in the freezer as I work on my attitude!

The Rev. Marty Hedgpeth

I recently heard a powerful witness to Christ's intervention into someone's life through prayer. I am always excited to hear such accounts of miracles in our modern world, but my joy in this account was cut short. I may have misunderstood the presenter, but I understood him to say that God's interaction in our lives was related to our belief and faith in God. I understood him to say that if we had **enough** faith, God would answer any prayer that we asked of God. I disagree greatly with that point of view.

We often proclaim as a Church that we are saved by faith, and I hold this to be a foundational truth in our relationship with God. What I also hold to be true, however, is that it is not **our** faith through which we are justified or saved, but the faith of **our savior,** Jesus Christ. All that we have been given from God, including our life itself, is a gift of pure grace. All that we will receive from God in the future, including our redemption and everlasting life, will be a gift of pure grace, completely devoid of any relationship to what we have done or left undone.

If we feel a need to try to link God's response to our needs and prayers to our faith, I would suggest we make the connection in the needs and prayers that we perceive were **not** answered by God. Don't stay awake at night worrying whether your faith is strong enough for God to answer your prayers and keep your children safe at school. Instead, try pondering a faith that is strong enough to continue to trust in the goodness of God in the midst of tragedy.

Our God is not all powerful AND loving. Our God is all powerful IN loving. God loves us perfectly when we lie and cheat and steal. God loves us perfectly when we are stricken with AIDS and cancer and disease. God loves us perfectly when we refuse to acknowledge God's existence or when we only call on Him to curse His name. Perfect love does not require anything from the beloved, but continues without limit, simply desiring to be loved in return.

The Rev. John Porter-Acee

In August, one of my great mentors died at age 94, completely at peace, eager to see Jesus (which he mentioned often in his last week), and surrounded by all his children. I'm sure his death was so grace-filled, in part, because he was a great man of prayer.

Prayer is being with God, silently and in conversation. It is the source of an honest and true relationship with God. And as much as we may pray while driving, at meetings, organizing our children, or exercising, true prayer requires stillness and quiet, for in that silent emptiness we can simply be ourselves rather than do anything. Another great man of prayer, Thomas Merton, has written, "We are warmed by fire, not by the smoke of the fire. We are carried over the sea by a ship, not by the wake of a ship. So too, what we are is to be sought in the invisible depths of our own being, not in our outward reflection in our own acts. We must find our real selves not in the froth stirred up by the impact of our being upon the beings around us, but in our own soul which is the principle of all our acts." We must reclaim ourselves as human beings, not human doings.

Nothing is more important for us as disciples than prayer. My mentor loved to quote Pascal who once wrote, "All the troubles of life come upon us because we refuse to sit quietly for awhile in our rooms." Claim 5-10 minutes a day, sit quietly, allow yourself to simply be with God, discover how God is with you in the stillness, and over time, simple and surprising things will happen.

The Rev. Marty Hedgpeth

The new season of American Idol started last night, and I admit to being a fan of the show. The show's musical director, Rickey Minor, has written an autobiography entitled, "There's No Traffic on the Extra Mile." Apparently he credits his own rags to riches story to plain old hard work. The book's title caught my attention and led me to look up the related passage from Matthew's Gospel: "Whoever forces you to go one mile, go with him two." (Matt. 5:41)

The circumstances of our economy have certainly "forced" many of us, if not all of us, to go a direction we did not and would not choose. But both the title of Minor's book and Jesus' words from the Sermon on the Mount that Matthew gives us, suggest that when we are **forced** to walk a mile in one direction, choosing also to go the additional mile can lead us to new opportunities for growth, service and deeper discipleship. Owning fewer things might give way to being in richer relationships. More time might translate into less fragmentation of our lives.

During the last recession, Apple Inc. spent time researching and developing new products ideas: the iPod and iTunes. When the recession ended, Apple was in prime market position for success. If we, as individuals and a congregation, have been forced to walk a mile we did not choose, perhaps we can also walk the extra, and often less trafficked, mile -- invest more energy into family, friendships, and communities of support. Embrace change and innovation at work, home and in our spiritual life. Learn a new skill; acknowledge and strengthen our talents. Resist holding back and give selflessly. The extra mile nearly always brings us to places of greater wholeness and peace.

Lisa +

With the dawn of e-mail came a whole new world of jokes and clever pictures, stories, and ideas. Sometimes I get so many of these, I just have to push the delete button in order to have a life. But I'll admit I do read my fair share. Yesterday I got one that I enjoyed, and it does have a point regarding faith journeys.

A 5th grade teacher in a Christian school asked her class to look at TV commercials and see if they could use them in some way to communicate ideas about God. Here are the results:

God is like Ford -- he has a better idea. God is like Coke -- he is the real thing. God is like Hallmark Cards -- he cares enough to send the very best. God is like Tide -- he gets the stains out that others leave behind. God is like General Electric -- he brings good things to life. God is like Scotch Tape -- you can't see him, but he's there. God is like Delta -- he's ready when you are. God is like VO-5 Hairspray -- he holds through all kinds of weather. God is like Dial Soap -- aren't you glad you have him? Don't you wish everybody did?

Yes, these are very clever, but the great point is that when we actually pay attention and try to find God connections in our everyday lives, they are there in overwhelming abundance, and not just in television commercials. Take time to pay attention and look for God in your ordinary days. I think you'll find that the ordinary is brimming over with signs of our good God.

The Rev. Marty Hedgpeth

Over the past several days, I have been engaged in one of my least favorite tasks, the task of moving-packing up boxes of hefty theological tomes (some of which I have never read and probably never will), deleting computer files, cleaning out cabinets, wrapping icons, crosses and pictures in the bubble wrap where they will live until they find a new home on the walls of my new office. I must confess that I find all this activity abhorrent. Being from Mississippi, I have an inbred resistance to change. "If only things could stay the same," I think. "If only I never had to say goodbye to people and places that I love. If only I never had to adjust to new ways of acting and being." I find myself feeling this way even though the reasons for my current move are the happiest ones imaginable.

I know that I am not alone in my discomfort with change and transition. In a culture of constant upheaval, swapping familiar routines for new ones can be profoundly unsettling. Where to find solace in a society in which so little is constant? We Christians often look to our faith as a sort of fortress against what the Prayer Book calls "the swift and varied changes of the world." This is one of the reasons why there tend to be such strong, and often negative, reactions to any proposed alterations in the Church. Church, we suppose, ought to be a place as comfortable as a well-worn recliner, as predictable as a meal of meatloaf and mashed potatoes -- a place where we can go to take a break from the chaos and uncertainty of the outside world.

Certainly, church should be a place where we can go to feel safe and loved in the midst of life's storms. It should have an aura of the familiar. But if we assume that our faith is only about standing still, only about being comfortable, then we are bound to be disappointed. Even the most cursory reading of Holy Scripture makes clear that an essential characteristic of true faith is a decided openness to movement and transition. Throughout the Old Testament, God's chosen people are almost always on the go. Constantly, God asks them to stretch themselves, to try out new behaviors, to risk journeying into distant lands. Jesus' disciples, likewise, are a group always being pushed by their Master to explore uncharted territory, to take the message of salvation to people who have never heard it.

Changes in the Church abound these days (actually, they always have). We Christians cannot stand still forever but must, as St. Paul once put it, "press on." The good news is that we will not make our journey alone. Jesus will be with us at every step. The One who went all the way to Calvary for us will be beside us, behind us and before us, guiding us on the paths of righteousness and peace, making us lie down in green pastures and leading us beside still waters.

May God's richest blessings be yours as you continue venturing into God's new day. Please pray for me as I will pray for you.

The Rev. Julia Boyd

One of my favorite prayers is from St. Augustine and goes: "Lord, you have made us for yourself and our hearts are restless till they find their rest in you." I love that prayer because it is a constant reminder that we have been made to "run" on God. I was reminded of this during our mission trip to Costa Rica.

The bishop's wife let me watch her make guacamole -- it is the best I have ever had. And I was surprised when she took a couple of the avocado seeds and plopped them into the big bowl of guacamole. When I asked why she did that, she said that the seeds prevent the dip from turning brown -- a handy culinary tip, but also a good picture of life. Without the center of our life we wander and wither in all sorts of ways. But when we always have that center, we remain fresh and alive.

One day one of our projects was to remove a huge stump from the back yard. One young adult said we'd have it out in an hour. Eight hours later, all 22 of us were finally pulling it out of the ground. It was another good picture of life. When we are rooted and grounded in God's love, even when it seems that we are nothing but a stump, we are alive because of the source of our life.

Look around your life and see what kind of pictures are there to help you know and believe that your relationship with God is the most important thing in your life because it gives you life.

The Rev. Marty Hedgpeth

Edward Hays is a priest, trained by Benedictine Monks, and a self-titled folk artist and writer. One of the books he has written is a collection of parables called "The Ethiopian Tattoo Shop." In the parable of "The Fig Tree" there is a discourse between a gardener and a young fig tree. The young tree does not feel that being a fig tree would be very special or exciting, so the young tree has been trying its whole life to be something other than a fig tree. As you may guess, the tree has failed over and over again.

The gardener goes on to explain to the tree the difference between a job and a vocation. The gardener even gives the following quote from E. E. Cummings to the tree to think about:

"To be nobody but yourself in a world which is doing its best, day and night, to make you everybody else, means to fight the hardest battle which any human being can fight, and never stop fighting."

The story ends with the little fig tree saying in a loud and confident voice of self-resolution, "I think I'll be a fig tree."

What a wonderful gift parables are. Parables can take questions as complicated as "What is my purpose in life?" and shed a bit of light on them. I invite you to spend some time now, or later today, or this week, and think about what type of tree you might be. We laugh at the proposition of a fig tree trying to grow apples, but yet we find it somewhat shocking or embarrassing when we cannot always produce the fruit that we might desire to produce. Take some time to think about how uniquely you have been made and what a gift it might be to the world to be blessed with you exactly as you are with no masks, walls, or excuses.

Psalm 139: 13-18

"For it was you who formed my inward parts;
    you knit me together in my mother's womb.
I praise you, for I am fearfully and wonderfully made.

Wonderful are your works;
    that I know very well.
My frame was not hidden from you,
    when I was being made in secret,
    intricately woven in the depths of the earth.
Your eyes beheld my unformed substance.
In your book were written
    all the days that were formed for me,
    when none of them as yet existed.
How weighty to me are your thoughts, O God!
How vast is the sum of them!
I try to count them -- they are more than the sand;
I come to the end -- I am still with you."

In Christ,

The Rev. John Porter-Acee III

Recently I traveled to Orkney, a group of islands in Scotland that lie to the north of John O'Groats. It is a wild and woolly place, but in the midst of the islands is a huge body of calm, deep water, Scapa Flow, which served as the Royal Naval Base in both world wars. During World War II a number of Italian prisoners of war were taken to Orkney to build barriers on the east side of Scapa Flow to keep out invading Germans. Nothing could have been more different from Italy than Orkney and yet the Italians made their compound as homey as possible. One thing was lacking -- a chapel.

Finally two small Quonset huts were put up and the Italians set about making the space holy. It is quite an experience to be driving in Scotland (and not far from Norway) and to see a little chapel with an ornate façade standing by the sea and an Italian flag waving in the breeze. Inside the walls are painted in such a way that you truly believe there are stone walls and carvings, arches and apses. It was one of the holiest chapels I have ever been in, not so much because of the transformed space, but because of the faith of the men who did the transformation.

Speaking at the rededication of the chapel in 1960, the priest said, "In the heart of human beings the truest and most lasting hunger is for God." It was so for those displaced Italians. It was so for some Charlotteans who couldn't afford to use gas rations to get uptown for church during World War II. In their hunger for God, they established this parish and began in a Quonset hut. On Orkney in the Italian Chapel, I said a prayer of thanksgiving for our founding members.

And I had another prayer which was for us as a parish. I prayed that in our hunger for God, we might be led to do great things that are as transformative as that little hut in a wild and woolly part of the world and as the little hut that has become this great parish. But each of us must ponder individually, "What will I do with my hunger for God?" There are millions of ways to satisfy that hunger from deeper worship and study to greater service and compassion. Find your way and you will be transformed.

The Rev. Marty Hedgpeth

Last week twenty of us gathered around a table at Christ Church for More than Lunch. We talked about the challenges and blessings of life transitions, specifically in these difficult economic times. One woman, whose family had been through job loss and financial upheaval several years ago, said she focused then on giving to her children things that no one could ever take away from them.

I loved what she said and have been reflecting on it. My husband and I have given our children many tangible gifts that "moth and rust consume," but the most important gifts are those that cannot be taken away, no matter their or our circumstances. Do our children have gifts of resilience and hope and faith within them to transcend disappointment and failure? Do they see themselves as precious and worthy of self-respect as well as respect from others? Do they know how to be a friend and make a friend? Did we encourage and foster a spirit of compassion in them?

A few weeks ago I heard Rabbi Sandy Eisenberg Sasso of Indianapolis interviewed on the radio program "Speaking of Faith." She spoke directly to this task of giving our children things no one can take away from them: "I think society does a very good job in teaching us how to be consumers and a very good job in teaching us how to be competitors. The question I think parents are struggling to answer is how do we not just teach our children's minds, but how do we teach their souls? And that's a much deeper question. And I know we want our children to be more than consumers and competitors. We want something much more. We want our children to be gracious and grateful. We want them to have courage in difficult times. We want them to have a sense of joy and purpose. And that's what it means to nurture their spiritual lives."

No matter the age of our children -- no matter our own age -- the nurture and care of our spiritual lives is critical to our own health and wholeness and to all those whose lives touch ours.

Peace to all,
Lisa

For the past four weeks, I have co-led a class on Celtic spirituality with Zibbie Allen. It has been a joy and a blessing to me in many ways. One of the most helpful things for me has been coming to a deeper understanding of the constant presence of God. The Celts had a prayer for everything -- getting out of bed, washing one's face, setting the fire, milking the cow, walking to work, guiding one's ship, and getting undressed at night. Every moment in life was full of the possibility of the holy for the Celts. This is certainly something that we could all use more of in our modern daily lives.

The other most helpful thing I have learned from the ancient Celts is a greater appreciation of the Trinity. We tend to think of one person of God at a time, while the Celts were constantly aware of all three persons surrounding them. In some very real ways this idea has tripled my thinking of God. And it is true that the more we live in awareness of our good God's presence, the greater will be our sense of peace.

So try a Celtic view one day. Say a little prayer about all the little things you do each day -- from brushing your teeth to carpooling; from driving in Charlotte traffic to sitting through one more swim meet. And remember that God is with you in far more ways than you can imagine.

"The God of life with guarding hold you,
The loving Christ with guarding fold you,
The Holy Spirit, guarding, mold you,
each night of life to aid, enfold you,
each day and night of life uphold you."

The Rev. Martha Hedgpeth

I am reading a great book entitled "Messy Spirituality: God's Annoying Love for Imperfect People" by Michael Yaconelli. I love the title! In the book, Yaconelli addresses all the "I don'ts" we often say and feel that lower our self-esteem and steal our joy: "I don't pray enough, I don't read my bible enough, I don't...enough." The unfortunate conclusion that results is the overall feeling of "I must not be a very good Christian." Ever felt this way before? It is awful to feel that we do not measure up in God's eyes. As Parker Palmer once wrote, "there is no greater punishment than participating in our own diminishment."

Now, lest you think I am suggesting it doesn't matter whether we engage in disciplines that draw us to God, let me say this: we ought to strive to live deeply with God. The ancient bishop Tertullian wrote in the 3rd century, "God's greatest joy is a human being fully alive." When we live with God in prayer, worship, and service, God participates in our lives and helps us to reach our full potential.

But, God's love doesn't begin when we reach our full potential. It begins in the messiness of our lives. Our messiness is the foundation in which God's work is done. God is never repelled by us. As Paul Tillich wrote, "the greatest challenge is to accept the fact that we have already been accepted."

Are you willing to give in to God's outrageous, indiscriminate love?

The Rev. Chip Edens

A couple of weeks ago when my Newsweek arrived I immediately turned to the last page to read "The Last Word" by Anna Quindlen. We're about the same age, I've been reading her work since about 1980, and I agree with about 95% of what she says. I was saddened to read that she is giving up her Newsweek column. I was horrified to read that she was giving it up because in judging a journalism contest, she realized that the next generation was extremely thoughtful and capable and that it was time for her to step aside. I thought how sad that her last column fell in the 5% of her work with which I disagree. And then this past Sunday happened.

It was Youth Sunday and with the flourishing of our youth program, this place was crawling with young people. I heard four of them preach in the Church, three of them read, two of them do the Prayers of the People, and I saw a few administer chalices, many serve as acolytes, and quite a few serve as ushers. I wasn't struck so much by the flawless execution of their roles, but I was deeply moved by their faith and the caring community they have created. Then I was at a gathering that evening where a group of our teens unveiled a website (created by one of our young women) that is a project of theirs -- raising money to complete a computer lab in Costa Rica in honor of one of their group, Greer Yorke, who died tragically last year. Whether you contribute to it or not, go look at www.greeryorke.webs.com and you will see some extraordinary young people.

Anna Quindlen was right, as usual. If you want to feel good about the future of the Church and the future of our faith, stop a young person and have a conversation. You will discover as I did what a joy and honor it is to be in community with them; like me, you may have your faith strengthened by theirs; and you certainly will discover that whenever we decide to step aside, the light of Christ will burn just as brightly through these brilliant young Christians.

The Rev. Marty Hedgpeth

I recently got an email from a longtime, faithful parishioner who felt I had abused the responsibility that I so delicately hold in the pulpit of this (or any) church. While I disagree with some of his points, it is still a welcomed letter. Since I understood his purpose to be "speaking the truth in love," it was easier for me to try to learn from his comments than to try to ignore them.

In retrospect, I think that I was indeed guilty of preaching a sermon that could have been received as one-sided. Defining a conflict and then claiming that God is on one side or the other is a very popular way to speak in the church, it seems. I, however, tend to see no use for that technique. I firmly believe that God is passionately for some actions that are taken everyday, and I firmly believe that God is passionately against some actions of the day as well. What then are we to do as Christians? Are we to guess at the truth and then tell others that they must follow our assumptions? No. Are we to always compromise, admitting that there is no way to be sure and hence no reason to be passionate? Of course not. What then?

We must seek God in all that we do. We must try to live our lives according to the Gospel as we struggle to understand it. We must try to straighten the ways that we perceive are crooked and raise up those that we see as the lowly. We must not assume that our side is the only side that God is active on. We must not even assume that our side is the side that God is more pleased with. We must pray that we may have the grace to do God's will in the midst of our ignorance.

Benedicta Ward writes "The message of the gospel in the person of Christ is universal or it is nothing." I think that Ward is right. As frustrating as it may be for us as we strive for answers that are clear and effective right now, God is not often as interested in the short term as we are. "The Gospel Truth" can be said to support almost any action and any side of any argument, but that doesn't mean that we have to think that way or preach that way. The REAL TRUTH, without the scare quotes, is that our God is a loving and good God, and that in the end, He wins.

The Rev. John Porter-Acee

I love the Olympics. The Games are now a week old and I am feeling the effects of sleep-deprivation as I stay up way too late each night to see various contests. I love seeing individuals who are truly focused on being their very best and who willingly test themselves against others who are equally gifted.

But my favorite part of the Olympics is watching the parents of the athletes. They unsuccessfully try not to look as if all of the pressure in the world is on them and not their competing children. They try not to reveal that their hearts are in their throats and they are dying a thousand deaths as their children perform before the world. They exude love and pride when their children finish, no matter how they finish -- first or last.

The point is that God is that kind of parent for each and every one of us. In the great movie, "Chariots of Fire," Eric Liddell explains to his sister his delay in doing mission work in China in order to run in the Olympics by saying, "God made me fast and when I run I feel his pleasure." God has fearfully and wonderfully made each one of us, unique and gifted in our own way. And whenever we are truly ourselves, seeking to be our best, God in heaven is bursting with anticipation, pride, and joy regardless of the outcome. Watch the Games and notice the parents and then imagine God as that parent to you. It will change your relationship with God and it will give you confidence to try amazing things.

The Rev. Marty Hedgpeth

If I could tell everyone in the entire world one thing, I would make sure all people know that God loves them. If I had two things that I could tell the world, the second one would be that we are all in this together. God created each and every one of us as individuals with unique and tremendous talents, but God also created us to live in community with each other.

One of the most misunderstood pieces of scripture was written to lead us to a deeper understanding of how powerful our community should be. Unfortunately, it has been used to try to encourage the individual instead of the community. In Paul's first letter to the Corinthians, he writes "God is faithful, and he will not let you all be tested beyond your strength, but with the testing he will also provide the way out so that you all may be able to endure it." (1 Corinthians 10:13) The limits of our English lead this verse to be mistranslated into the singular "you" and over and over again this verse is used as a pep talk for someone in crisis. If we lived as God intended there would never be "someone" in crisis. The community of believers would "bear all things, believe all things, hope all things, endure all things" together! (1 Corinthians 13:7) Know that God loves you. Know that we were created to live this life together. If you are hurting, allow the community to care for you. If you are well, seek the one who could benefit from the marvelous gifts that you have to offer them and let them know that you all will make it through this together.

The Rev. John Porter-Acee +

Exactly a year ago I was spending the first part of my sabbatical in Scotland and the first part of that trip was a retreat on Lindisfarne, Holy Island. In recalling that amazing time there, I have been rereading a little book of reflections and prayers by Ray Simpson, a priest who runs a retreat house on the island. One of my favorite places on Lindisfarne was the Heugh, a grassy hill with a sharp cliff dropping down to the beach, a high spot from which you can gain the best perspective on the island. In writing of this spot, Simpson says:

"When we are at the edge we see horizons which are denied to those who stay in their comfort zones. God likes to take us to the edges. Often it is only when we are willing to go to the edges that we truly meet others, for many people who are on the edges of loneliness, anger, despair or adventure recognize and reach out to others who are also an edge. Jesus allowed himself to be pushed to the edges of society. That is why he could communicate to so many ordinary people. This is how the truly precious things of life are passed on -- at the edges."

I love the mixture of total fear and exhilarating awe that I get peering over high windy cliffs in Scotland. If I can remember that feeling when called out of my comfort zone by Jesus, I will be a better disciple. How is Jesus calling you out of your comfort zone? It just may be that following our Lord out to some edges, to some scary places may be just the place where we may reach out to others or have them reach out to us and in that encounter we meet the living God. Follow Jesus ... out to the edges.

The Rev. Martha Hedgpeth

When Willie, a miniature schnauzer, was lost in a blizzard, I was ten years old and prayed to God to bring him home safely. Sometime after midnight, he scratched at the back door, and my mother (who had slept downstairs on the sofa so she could hear him if he showed up in the middle of the night) welcomed an ice-caked Willie to home and hearth. That's often how ten-year-olds pray -- by asking God to break through the clouds and do us personal favors.

Prayer is not only a trade tool of mine but part of my private life as well. I haven't stopped asking God for personal favors, but I have stopped believing that's how prayer, or God, works. Scripture tells us Jesus prayed. A lot. And when he asked God for a personal favor (remove this cup from me), his request was not granted. I don't see prayer as our way to God but as God's avenue to reach us. Prayer is the avenue through which the Holy Spirit works within us and through us and for us. Effective prayer is not about changing God's mind or convincing God to be merciful or loving; effective prayer changes our minds and empowers us to be merciful and loving.

But what about intercessory prayer -- when we pray for someone else's health, happiness or safety? Is God measuring our prayers before doling out healing or providing hope to another? I believe that we are the channels of God's grace in this world, and that prayer helps to unclog us, and the flow of love, forgiveness, hope and healing (not necessarily curing) through us and onward into the world. When we pray we place ourselves in such a way that we are nearer to God, more available to receive and pass on God's peace and strength for living and for dying.

I suppose it's a little like my mother sleeping on the couch that wintry night -- she set herself a little closer to the possibility of hope, to being able to hear another's cry for help and to respond. And in a way I can't fully explain, knowing my mother's slept on the couch that night, drew me closer to God's hope and care as well. When someone prays for me, it feels the same.

I'll still go on asking God for personal favors because it's one way I stay honest with God. But most of all I pray that my ideas for health and happiness don't get in the way of God's clear, bright purposes for wholeness and meaning in my life and in the lives of others.

Lisa Saunders

This past Sunday as I gave a Communion wafer to a young boy named William, he took the bread that I offered and then very politely said, "Thank you." I smiled and continued down the altar rail to his mother. After I had given her the bread, however, my thoughts caught up to me, and I quickly leaned back to William and said, "You are very welcome!"

How often do you hear the words "You are welcome"? You probably hear them enough that you don't really think about the full meaning of what you are hearing. You may not even think about the meaning of what you are saying when you use those words. I considered it a privilege to use those words this past Sunday, a privilege and a very important part of my relationship with young William.

I know that it is our social custom to say "you are welcome" when someone says "thank you," but that is not the important part of my relationship with William. What is important is for William, and all of the rest of us, to know that WE ARE WELCOME!! No matter who we are, what we have done, how we feel, or what we have to offer, we are truly welcomed by God. I'm not trying to start a discussion about who should receive communion; I'm trying to do something that I feel is a fundamental part of being a priest of the Church, and that is to proclaim God's unequivocal welcome to all of creation.

God wants us all. God wants to consume us all with his abundant love at every instant. God wants all parts of us, too. Even the dark and scary parts of us are welcomed into his unbounded love. William, I hope you could hear me and that you might come to understand that you, and the rest of us, are indeed very welcome.

The Rev. John Porter-Acee

While watching a baseball game this past week, I heard one of the announcers recalling the opportunity he had to watch Ozzie Smith, a Hall of Fame shortstop, at practice. He said Ozzie could field ground balls at short, and then blindly throw the ball to first base without ever taking his eyes of the third baseman, with whom he was holding an intense conversation. I was impressed by his story but I was not surprised in the slightest.

Ozzie was great, and the only way to be a great baseball player is to practice every piece of the game until you can "do it with your eyes closed." Even your thoughts have to become reflexes instead of decisions. You can't choose to swing at a 98 mile an hour fastball. You either swing or you don't. While chasing a ball to the wall in the outfield you don't have time to turn around and decide which base you should throw it to. You just turn and fire based on the meticulous habits you have created in your mind and muscles; habits to evaluate the speed of the base runners, the velocity of the ball, the time it took for you to arrive, the distance your throw will have to cover, and so forth and so on. None of the miracles that happen on the baseball diamond could happen without practicing until the game is just an extension of who you are.

So why go on about baseball? Faith is exactly the same way. In baseball we practice catching, throwing, hitting and running. To strengthen our faith, we practice worship, service, fellowship and study. The Hall of Fame Christians have done this until their meticulously practiced habits have simply become an extension of who they are and miracles happen. The act of worship has to become a part of who you are so that you don't have to decide to be in awe of God but instead live in constant wonder and thanksgiving. It is one thing to choose to go and serve others in a soup kitchen, but practice allows you to lead a life of service. Anyone could compliment a friend, but it takes a Hall of Famer to have the kind of Christian fellowship that builds up the Body of Christ and brings out the best in others. We can all read the Bible, but we can also all choose to devote ourselves to the teachings of the Apostles and immerse ourselves in the wisdom of the Church.

We may not all have the genes to be professional athletes, but we have all been created to love God, care for each other, and serve the world. Just like Ozzie Smith, there is much work for us to do for our potential to be met. Just like Ozzie Smith, most of that work is not done in the spotlight of prime time television. Instead, the preparation happens in our homes, classrooms, offices, and church pews. Countless repetitions are necessary to improve, even the slightest bit in some areas, but if we stick with it there will be a day that we "do it with our eyes closed."

The Rev. John Porter-Acee

Every time a group of this parish goes to Bay St. Louis, Mississippi to do post-Katrina reconstruction, I like to take a little time to go sit in the Memorial Garden at Christ Episcopal Church (where we stay). It is a beautiful spot, right at the edge of the beach, looking out at the bay. Under a huge live oak, there are tablets that name the saints of that parish who are buried there. There is a simple wooden altar and wooden benches and some simple plants, but mostly there is the live oak tree. When Katrina struck, this was the first tree to be engulfed by the raging sea. There was great concern that these massive trees would not survive being buried under 30 feet of sea water. After the storm, they all looked like skeletons and many died. But this one, at the heart of the memorial garden, is now displaying more and more green leaves and sheltering the saints who rest under its increasingly shady branches. It is a gentle, simple, and awesome sign of resurrection.

Our lives seem engulfed by danger, darkness, and death in many ways -- hostilities abound in the world; natural disasters are more violent and frequent; economies slip, slide, and crumble; jobs are less secure or gone in an instant; and events in individual lives seem out of our control. But we must not lose hope because our faith promises that our good God is living and active and able to bring new life to every situation, no matter how bleak. Like that live oak tree, it may take lots of time, but resurrection happens. In your own life, no matter what your situation, remember that live oak tree and be on the lookout for the signs of new life and hope that are and will spring forth.

The Rev. Marty Hedgpeth

About the Authors

The Clergy of Christ Episcopal Church, Charlotte, North Carolina, are the authors of the devotions collected in this anthology. In experience, they range from a beloved priest who has led congregations all over the United States to a recent seminary graduate who had just been ordained. They are all gifted writers who share remarkable insights about their shared Christian faith.

LaVergne, TN USA
23 November 2010
205940LV00001B/2/P